THE
Signature
SERVICE
STRATEGY

Richard Solomon

D0881627

Copyright © 2018 Richard Solomon

All rights reserved. No part of this publication may be reproduced, distributed, or transmitted in any form or by any means, including but not limited to photography, recording, or other electronic or mechanical methods, without the prior written permission of the publisher, except in the case of brief quotations embodied in critical reviews and certain other noncommercial uses permitted by copyright law. For permission requests, contact the publisher at the information below.

Development Consulting Center Limited
11 Richard Lane
Southern Main Road Cunupia,
Trinidad and Tobago.
info@dccintl.com
www.dccintl.com
1-868-222-5104

Ordering Information:
Quantity sales. Special discounts are available on quantity purchases by corporations, associations, and others. For details, contact the publisher at the addresses above.

Publisher: Development Consulting Center Limited
Cover designed by: Bogdan Matei – Bucharest, Romania
Editing by: Douglas Williams – New Castle, USA
Infographics and Tables by: Daval Dodiya – Ahmedahbad, India
Layout: Richa Bargotra, Panchkula, India

The Signature Service Strategy: How to Create a Super CRM Machine/Richard Solomon

ISBN: 978-976-96134-0-9 (pbk)
ISBN: 978-976-96134-1-6 (ebook)

1. The main category of the book – Customer Service – Another category – 2. Customer Experience – Other categories - 3. Strategy – 4. Hiring – 5. Empowerment 6. Organization Development – 7. Leadership – 8. Training – 9. Organization and workplace Culture

Printed in the United States

First Edition

10 9 8 7 6 5 4 3 2 1

Dedication

This book is firstly dedicated to my wife and biggest supporter - Shelly-Ann and our two brilliant and beautiful daughters Danielle and Shantel.

Secondly, to my many clients the world over who continue to provide me with opportunities to share, learn and grow.

Richard Solomon

Table of Contents

Richard Solomon

Richard Solomon

Richard Solomon

Richard Solomon

Preface

Great customer service is the best strategy any business could possibly have. If your organization is like most, the service quality is not nearly where your customers want it to be. Most likely you see the telltale signs of poor customer reviews, complaints, churn or lower than expected sales numbers. Maybe the cost of selling has increased or your competitors are gaining ground. These all trace back to service.

Presumably you have made or seen various efforts at improving service within your organization. Many see service as being the domain of the "customer service department," and others believe that an annual training event will suffice. Neither of these approaches is sufficient nor do they work.

I like many have complained about the quality of service somewhere, at some time and we have all walked away from a company – choosing instead to complain with our feet, possibly defecting to the competition in hopes that, by some stroke of heavenly blessing, things will be better on the other side (good luck with that).

I have been fortunate to travel to many places and observe peoples, cultures and companies in more than 36 countries. There are the small organizations that operate on little islands in the Caribbean – like Anguilla and St. Kitts and Nevis and Grenada, where populations are so small that it is very likely that you may have known

Richard Solomon

your co-worker before you or they came to the company. Then there are the mega-companies sitting on one of the continents or in large population centers where you can work for a company and never know someone sitting one or two floors above, including New York, Washington D.C., Johannesburg, and London.

As a trainer, coach, keynote speaker, change architect, consultant, student of human behavior, and a customer, I have been on the receiving end of (what I call) "tripping-over-themselves service." But I have also received the kind that left me SMH in disbelief. Over my career, I have noticed that some companies are extremely good at delighting the customer, while others are just horrible, with most falling somewhere in between.

For the last 20 years, I have provided consulting services to hundreds of companies around the globe, including some of the *Fortune* 500. I have a simple brain; I break things down to their simplest components, and really have no interest in *complexifying* (yes, I know it's not an actual word) anything. I have helped companies transform themselves and build service cultures that have directly impacted the bottom line and satisfaction of customers.

This book pulls together my decades of global experience. My intent is to give you hope and present a practical process that can be used to change your organization into becoming a Super CRM machine that delivers **signature** service to all customers.

"**Signature** service" is the highest level of service a company can deliver; to create it, the organization has to live its best life on many fronts. The payoffs are multi-level and powerful, for this is one journey where everyone wins. The results of this journey? Better leadership, employee engagement, attitudes, processes, products, customer experience, quality, efficiency, sales, and profits. A journey to a **signature** service culture is one worth the effort, and most companies are already doing many of the things needed. Streamlining and alignment are your friends.

Broadly, this book is written for anyone interested in improving service quality within their organization. But specifically, if you are an entrepreneur, own a business, or manage people who serve customers, if you are the CEO, COO, CPO (Chief People Officer), CCO (Chief Customer Officer), then this book is definitely for you!

You will find three things throughout these pages: **Why, What** and **How**! This is meant to be a guidebook that you can use to transform the culture of your own organization or department into one where **signature** service is the most important thing and everyone wins!

Lots of stories illustrate the points made, personally, I love stories and find them very instructive and entertaining. Pay close attention to the "What to do" section near the end of every chapter; they will guide you to the actions you need to take. Welcome aboard!

Richard Solomon

Chapter 1

The State of Service in the 21ˢᵗ Century

In my estimation, service quality in the 21ˢᵗ century is in a poor state for most companies. I know some are trying, but it's not enough. Few lights glimmer at the end of the tunnel and, for most, I am not even sure we can see the tunnel, let alone the lights. The giants and a few small and focused organizations stand way out front, doing amazing things that make us go "wow!" But generally, what passes for service is so sad that as many as **25 out of 26 dissatisfied customers don't even bother to complain[1]; they just leave!** Add to this, the fact that 2/3 of customers who leave an organization do so for a service related issues, and you have a very abysmal picture indeed.[2]

According to a 2014 American Express report on Global Customer Service, in most markets, less than 30 percent of consumers see an "increased focus on customer service" on the part of businesses in the current economy.[3]

Forgive me for asking the obvious, but didn't the start of the 21ˢᵗ century see a world in the throes of economic struggle? Wasn't there a global financial meltdown in 2007-2008 and aren't some economies

---

[1] (CSM 2016)
[2] (American Express 2010)
[3] (American Express 2014)

Richard Solomon

still working on a comeback? Aren't many economies still reeling under the pressure of high unemployment and austerity measures? Have we not seen the demise of a list of familiar names and others sitting on the edge? What about Circuit City, Washington Mutual Bank, and AMR Corporation (Parent company of American Airlines)? Aren't oil- and gas-dependent economies suffering from some the lowest prices in more than a decade? As a matter of fact, as I write this, Brent North Sea Crude oil is priced at 35.10 USD (January 2016) a barrel, while a similar amount of bottled water would cost around 120.00 USD. Talk about economic madness!

The fact is, in these hard times, customers have learned some tough lessons; they have had to do more with less and demand greater value for their money. This increased value requirement is not limited to the tangible – in fact, customers all over are demanding that you treat them better. As you will see throughout this book, countless examples show customers pressing organizations to raise the bar higher and higher to earn their business. In this case, service is most correctly recognized as true value.

The economic costs are sobering:

- On 23rd May 2012, the embattled tech giant Hewlett Packard unveiled a plan to slash 27,000 jobs, which was 8 percent of its worldwide workforce, by 2014. This was believed to be the third largest "workforce bloodletting" in tech history (behind IBM's 60,000 in 1993 and AT&T's 40,000 in 1995).[4]

---

[4] (Whittaker and Cheng 2012)

Richard Solomon

- Meg Whitman (HP CEO) oversaw the reduction of some 55,000 jobs at the tech giant, which is now being split in two for agility and efficiency. It has been a tough road.[5] Whitman herself has since departed HP (now Hewlett Packard Enterprise) as CEO although she will retain a seat on the Board of Directors.[6]

- According to several sources close to BlackBerry-maker Research in Motion (RIM), their troubles are only set to get worse, with as many as 6,000 jobs set to be cut as part of a major restructuring.[7]

- BlackBerry continues to see a fall in demand for their devices from 11.1 million in 2012, to 6 million in 2013, 3.4 million in 2014, .6 million in 2016.[8]

- On the other side of the pond (Atlantic Ocean), the story is no better I am afraid, with business failures still at unacceptable levels in the UK, Spain and Switzerland.[9]

- According to a 2017 report, the biggest risks for doing business globally are economic versus geopolitical, environmental, technological or societal.[10]

So bad is the business and service landscape that we recently saw four mobile phone companies fined a total of $7.3 million by regulators in Nigeria because of the poor quality of service.[11]

---

[5] (Egan 2015)
[6] (Vanian 2017)
[7] (Arthur 2012)
[8] (Moore 2017)
[9] (Dunn & Bradstreet Limited 2012)
[10] (World Economic Forum 2017)

Richard Solomon

With these challenging economic circumstances, you would think that companies would be *tripping over themselves* to make customers happy. Well, are they? No, they are not!

'We Want More!!!'

As customers in this century, we are the most demanding of all time – we want more, faster, better and cheaper in price. The iron triangle (as it is called in project management) indicates that you can't have all three of these (cheap, fast, and high-quality) simultaneously. What you must do is choose two: if it's cheap and high-quality, it won't be fast; if it's fast and high-quality, it won't be cheap; and if it's fast and cheap, it won't be high-quality. Getting all three is supposed to be impossible, I guess 21st century customers did not read that tweet!

Customers are very willing to trade in their old provider for another promising to deliver the goods and, more importantly, the service quality they want. Sixty four percent of customers switched suppliers in at least one industry due to poor service; that's 2 out of every 3.[12] More than this, there is a widening gap between service expectations on the part of customers and delivery on the part of service providers.

My theory is: As customers have become more aware of their rights, options and the experiences of fellow customers around the world, they have become emboldened to rightfully ask – hell, demand – more! At the same time, companies must respond to the potent expectations and demands of shareholders, suppliers, management,

---

[11] (Gambrell 2012)
[12] (Accenture 2011)

Richard Solomon

and employees, causing an already tenuous revenue pie to be cut into even more and thinner slices.

As world economies have progressed and more has become available, as new players have thrown their hats in the ring offering yet more products and services, as innovators and inventors have worked harder and faster to deliver even more, and as technology has spun insanely and sent us all on a blisteringly fast superhighway ride that no one could have imagined 25 years ago, we want more and we are not asking kindly. We are shouting, screaming, and demanding it — do it faster, better, and with greater value or we will find someone else who happily will (or at least they will promise and try).

And so, suppliers are redoubling their efforts to meet our insatiable appetites, happy to do almost anything to meet demand, since meeting such demand hits the bottom line in a great way. The effort, though, is slanted to products and service delivery versus customer service — focused on the *what* we want, but not so much concerned with the *how* it is delivered.

One of the obvious reasons that the supply chain has shifted eastward is the reduced cost of production, and skill availability. As economies like Japan and China are able to keep their cost of production comparatively low. Obviously, there are other reasons, but the need for healthier bottom lines has pushed many manufactures East. Go East Young Man! Naturally, we are seeing the negative impact of pushing eastward, as many suppliers pay inadequate attention to environmental sustainability (did someone say smog?) and poor working conditions have been highlighted as a major problem in some cases.

Richard Solomon

US President Barack Obama met with many business tycoons and tech giants during his presidency. In February 2011, Obama met with Apple's now deceased CEO Steve Jobs. Being his usual impatient, straight-talking self, Jobs displayed very little tolerance for bureaucratic sloth. When asked by Obama what it would take to bring certain jobs back to the USA (manufacturing iPhones and other products), Jobs' reply was unambiguous. "Those jobs aren't coming back," he said, according to another dinner guest.[13] People usually defer to the US president, but on this count, there would be no deference. Apple's executives find overseas workers to be flexible and diligent, and the cost is so much more advantageous to the company.

But somehow, the efforts to drive down the cost of production, increase quality, and widen margins are not being well-translated at most companies when it comes to service quality. How many companies can you name that are regularly tripping over themselves to exceed your quality of service expectations? If you are like me, the list is too short.

Let's do a comparison of demand in 2000 (the year America Online bought Time Warner for $16 billion)[14], 2010 (the year that Blockbuster filed for Chapter 11 bankruptcy)[15] and 2015 (the year that VW surpassed Toyota as the world's #1 automaker, the same year they were busted for rigging emissions tests).[16] If you recall, 2015 was also the year that Pfizer and Allergan reached a $149 billion deal to bring

---

[13] (Duhigg and Bradsher 2012)
[14] (ABC News 2009)
[15] (de la Merced 2010)
[16] (Hotten 2015)

Richard Solomon

Viagra and Botox under one corporate roof [17] ... interesting combination.

Demand Is Rising

Table 1 below compares sales of certain key products in the years 2000, 2010 and 2015. The figures tell a clear story; it says that the appetite of humanity for more stuff seems to be insatiable. What the figures don't reveal is the phenomenon of "luxury compression" – this is a situation where goods only previously available to the most affluent become available to the masses in a relatively short time. A great example is how smartphones (once only within the reach of mainly business managers and executives) are now available to every Sam, Bob and Beharry. Socialnomics' Erik Qualman shocked us all in 2013 when he boldly declared that more people owned a mobile phone than a toothbrush.[18] That which was recently considered luxury is now commonplace.

---

[17] (de la Merced 2015)
[18] (Qualman 2013)

Richard Solomon

SALES/USAGE	2000 (MILLIONS)	2010 (MILLIONS)	2015 (MILLIONS)
Cars	41	58.24	68.54
Mobile Phones	412	1596	1900
Personal Computers	134	346	238
Digital Cameras	11	109.9	42
Internet Users	401.18	2010	3220
Tablets	NA	15.32	217.4
Smartphones	.3	298	1424
Energy Consumption	10.1 Mtoe	13.14 Mtoe	15.1 Mtoe*

Table 1[19]

---

* Million Ton Oil Equivalent
[19] (Statista 2018; Gartner 2001; Statista 2017; Murphy and Roser 2018; Hughes 2015; Poushter 2016; energyfacaluty.com 2018)

Richard Solomon

You would notice when comparing 2010 with 2015 that there are two categories that regressed: there is a slowdown of about 10 percent in the personal computer category, and digital cameras have lost over 62 percent of the previous period's sales. Smartphones have enjoyed almost 210 percent growth. Some of the "smarts" in the smartphone are its ability to do much of what personal computers and digital cameras can do. The Internet is littered with reports showing how some of the losses in these areas contributed to the gains in another.

As Competition Increases

Surely you could see it coming; it only follows if we keep demanding more that well-intended, profit-minded, ambitious capitalists would find ways to deliver *that more*. In almost every industry, there has been unending growth in options, as more and more people, firms, and companies offer a variety of flavors and mixtures of products and services to satisfy this insatiable human consumptive hunger. Burger King has been telling us since the 1970s to *"have it your way,"* as well they should; after all, this place where growing demand exists is a perfect spot to let down the supply net, the result of which can be a nice catch of a wonderful thing called profit.

And so it is: The 20th century saw competitors being added apace, with the trend ramping up at the dawn of the 21st after a brief dip during the period 2007-2010. Take telecoms as a real example. In the Caribbean, the place I am lucky enough to call home *(yes, I live where you vacation)*, Cable and Wireless (a firm of British origin and a reminder of our days as Crown Colonies) had monopoly status by virtue of legislation, with the law written in such a way that it prevented other providers from entering the telecom markets in many

Richard Solomon

Caribbean countries for a very long time (over half a century in some cases). Cable and Wireless was secure in the knowledge that they would be the monopoly provider of telephony services on the islands.

But with the advent of wireless telephone technology, we saw an interesting move. In one case, Digicel, (now a global player) was able to snatch away more than half of C&W's wireless market share in 2 years!!! Can you imagine your company's plight if a competitor could simply walk into your back yard, wrestle you to the ground, and walk off with over 50 percent of your customers!!!??? Not a pretty sight, I assure you. To be fair, Cable and Wireless has reinvented itself, shed some of its weight and is now part of the TV and broadband giant Liberty Global.[20]

But the pie has grown; this competition and demand go together, as many Caribbean people walk around with two mobile phones, making the pie much bigger than it initially was. The rate of penetration has also expanded, with more and more users being added on a monthly basis. At the current time, the penetration rate in the Latin American region stands at around 72 percent.[21] Also, luxury compression has occurred in this industry, possibly faster than in any other, with mobile phones, smartphones and broadband being demanded at the deepest levels of society. That which was once luxury is now a necessity. As one client put it: broadband is no longer a nice-to-have; it is a utility like electricity or water!

Yet another example occurs in the domain of personal computing, Apple pioneered much of the technology used to bring computers to

---

[20] (Statista 2018)
[21] (GSM Association 2017)

Richard Solomon

us all. I remember a neighbor of mine having an Apple II with green letters (or maybe a green screen). For the life of me, I don't remember what the thing did exactly. What I do know is that we were all too happy and excited to play with it. But Apple lost their way (which they later found), and many new players came into the market. Fueled by consumer demand and technological advance, we have seen growth and explosion of a market that is too amazing to contemplate.

As we are on the topic of Apple, which you will see mentioned again and again in this book, I have always felt the comparison between a Mac and a PC was sort of strange, lots of people have made this comparison, almost as if a Mac is not a *PC*. Well if PC stands for Personal Computer (and it does), a technology championed by Apple anyway, then this nomenclature is off, it must be a misnomer. Don't get me wrong, I believe the comparison is useful from a user experience perspective, and I, like most people, have my preference (which I am not going to tell).

You don't have to look very far to find a plethora of options in almost any product category. The amount of brand names that surface in any category you identify is mind-boggling. Here is a list of competing brands by product/service category (Table 2) for your easy review.

Richard Solomon

PRODUCT CATEGORY	MANUFACTURER
Computers	acer · /ISUS COMPAQ DELL hp Lenovo TOSHIBA SONY SAMSUNG
Smartphones	· Google hTC LG MOTOROLA NOKIA RIM SAMSUNG SIEMENS SONY
Automobiles	Volkswagen NISSAN TOYOTA Audi ŠKODA BMW LAND ROVER SUZUKI SATURN mazda VOLVO MITSUBISHI KIA Ford GMC
Digital Cameras	Canon SONY Nikon PENTAX Panasonic CASIO SAMSUNG FUJIFILM
Athletic Wear	adidas THE NORTH FACE NIKE Columbia POLO UNDER ARMOUR
Household Appliances	GE SHARP Oster MAYTAG SAMSUNG BLACK& DECKER Hamilton Beach Magic Chef
Internet Service Providers	AT&T CABLE & WIRELESS COMCAST NETZERO verizon AOL virgin icuk
News	YAHOO! MSNBC USA TODAY BBC NEWS CNN abcNEWS NBC Google AP

Table 2

Richard Solomon

Of course, the crossovers among the categories and the brands are hard to miss; another factor in terms of competition is that companies have gone for organic and inorganic growth alike. Virgin is a great example of a multi-sector competitor; its empire spans banking, film, consumer electronics, commercial aviation, wellness, commercial space flight, travel, radio, TV, and many others. Go Sir Dick!!!

Informed and Connected

This is a period in time when people are more connected than ever before. There is so much more information being delivered today to all of humanity. But before we explore this, let's get behind the facts. There is an ever-reinforcing loop between information and technology, as each feeds the other and causes the next to increase. Paul Zane Pilzer first documented this concept in the groundbreaking book *Unlimited Wealth: The Theory and Practice of Economic Alchemy*. Pilzer was an economic advisor to both the Reagan and Bush (Senior) administrations and has had an amazing career in academia, banking, economics, as an author and entrepreneur.

At its base levels, technology improves how we process, store, configure, and retrieve information. But in fact, information is *the* key building block of technology (see Infographic 1 below). In the days of old, when someone thought they had invented something, had a new idea, or developed a radical approach, it was difficult to tell others. Sometimes it was quite dangerous, depending on your idea/discovery. For example, Copernicus is believed to have first proposed that the sun was at the center of the universe not the Earth, and he was almost

Richard Solomon

burned at the stake for his "heresy." Had he not recanted, he would have died for his beliefs.[22]

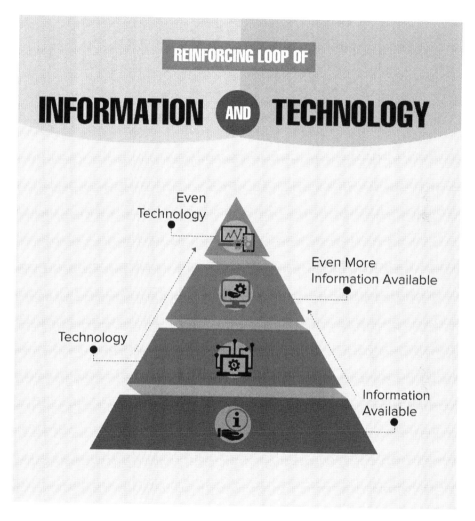

Infographic 1

In today's world, we are so wonderfully connected and far more open to other possibilities and ways of interpreting the world around us. Once we hit on an idea, discover some wonderful process or new

---

[22] (Pilzer 1990)

method, news quickly travels by binary code around the world at the speed of light (fiber optic cables), making it easy for others to adopt, build on our ideas, and enhance technology, which in turn feeds us more and more information. In fact, the number one language spoken on the planet is not English, Hindi, or Mandarin; the number one language spoken on planet Earth is binary, the various combinations of ones and zeros used 24 hours a day to keep humanity connected on a globe that never sleeps.

Think for a moment about what Apple has done with their App Store (I wonder if the use of the term "App" is for Apple or application? Hmmmmm...maybe both). Basically, what Apple did was create a platform (the I-ecosphere) upon which others could build, although they are continuously chided for being closed and controlling. Isn't it amazing how companies can resemble their founders – Steve Jobs is noted to have displayed some of these same characteristics in the biography of his life written by Walter Issacson.[23] Apple opened the I-ecosphere just enough to allow space for techno-creators the world over to bring dreams to life. And now, there's an app for that!

The uses for iOS devices is really only bound by human imagination, from having the daily newspaper delivered every morning, to being able to read a book seamlessly across all your devices, or paying for your favorite cup of java. Or just click on the compass and map app for directions, swipe left for a line level, or open the wallet app for your boarding pass. More complex applications in areas such as medicine, anthropology, and music creation are also

---

[23] (Isaacson 2011)

Richard Solomon

available at your fingertips. So successful has been the App Store that, not only have other platforms followed suit, but Apple has paid over 70B USD to app developers since the store was launched in 2008 as of this writing[24].

What we are seeing in terms of connectivity is only the tip of the iceberg. The Infographics below show predictions for 2020:

PREDICTIONS FOR 2020

---

[24] (Apple Inc. 2017b)

Richard Solomon

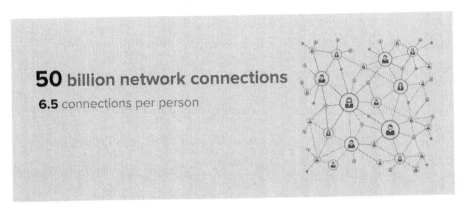

50 billion network connections: About 6.5 connections per person (assuming a world population of 7.6B).[25]

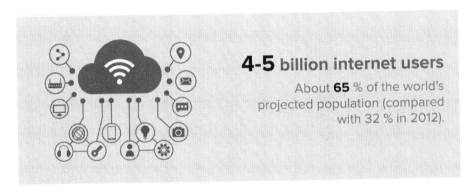

4-5 billion Internet **users:** About 65 percent of the world's projected population (compared with 32 percent in 2012).[26]

---

[25] (Tillman 2013)
[26] (Burgess 2015)

Richard Solomon

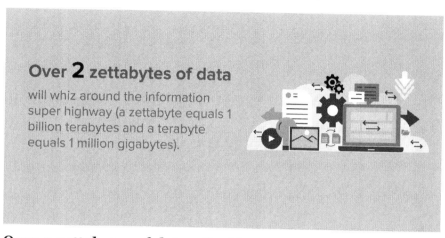

Over 2 zettabytes of data will whiz around the information super highway (a zettabyte equals 1 billion terabytes and a terabyte equals 1 million gigabytes).[27]

Fixed broadband speed will increase to 34 Mbps.[28]

---

[27] (Cisco 2017)
[28] (Cisco 2016)

Richard Solomon

Over half the world's Internet traffic is expected to come from Wi-Fi connections.[29]

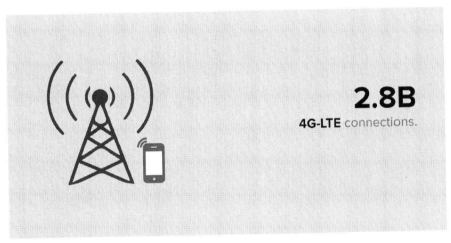

2.8B 4G-LTE connections.[30]

---

[29] (Cisco 2012)
[30] (Gilligan 2011)

Richard Solomon

24B devices will be connected to the Internet.[31]

814M global fixed-broadband subscribers.[32]

In fact, so insatiable is our data demand that one ATT executive predicts that they (AT&T) will begin offering "data only" cell phone plans soon.[33] Instead of getting minutes, you will get one big bundle of data. Remember the days when the Internet ran on the phone network? Well, it's the other way around now, as the phone systems run on the Internet (so to speak). Being more in the know amplifies

---

[31] (Malik 2011)
[32] (Point 2014)
[33] (Brodkin 2012)

Richard Solomon

customers' demand for quality, value, improved features, customization, speed, and better service.

The Perfect Storm

There was a time when your main competition would come from the store down the street or maybe a town or state over. Sure, foreign competition is not something new, but times have changed – oh how they have changed! Online retail sales account for about 12 percent of all retail sales if you factor out fuel, automobiles, restaurant and bar sales.[34] This figure has been on a steady growth path with no signs of letting up. Big names like Amazon, Apple and other e-tailers make it super-easy for customers. Traditional retail is actually on a downward trajectory, while the likes of Amazon are "eating the retail world," according to Rob Sanderson of MKM Partners. [35] Amazon alone accounts for about 43 percent of US online retail sales. Globally, ecommerce is projected to account for as much as 15 percent of retail sales by 2020.[36]

Amazon, Apple and other giants are the driving force, but you may have noticed some less-likely players getting into the ring. The social media giant Facebook cannot be described as an online retailer, but are they ever a facilitator! Gone are the days when you could have simply browsed your timeline without being marketed to – ads are everywhere and video is the medium of choice! Google has also increased e-marketing with their amazing ability to track your interests and desires. While these are not online retailers themselves,

---

[34] (Gesenhues 2017)
[35] (Thomas 2017)
[36] (Intelligence 2017; Statista 2017a)

Richard Solomon

they are what I have coined "e-tail e-enablers," those who make it easier and easier for buyers and sellers to meet and do business in the virtual marketplace.

The plot thickens simply by applying the laws of demand and supply; most brick-and-mortar businesses cannot compete on price with the online sellers. After all, if a customer came to your store, all he or she would get is your one price, but there is no shortage of options online. Also, because online retailers like Amazon don't just sell their own stock, they are effectively competing on multiple fronts; price, quality, convenience and even service.

E-tailers, and e-tail e-enablers do not tell the whole story. Many customers are just tired of the traditional retail headache. Not only does physical shopping take more effort and time (get dressed, drive, traffic, parking, people) if your customers are like many I have talked to, the online retail systems generally work well for them, and when they fail, the fix is so much easier than with brick-and-mortar options.

Globalization

What is it really and how does it impact service demand and delivery? Globalization is the giant invisible hand that pulls islands, nations, and continents "closer together" than ever before. It is the unseen force that makes it easy to order products designed in Cupertino, CA, manufactured at Foxconn in China, and have them delivered to your doorstep in (let's say) the Caribbean in a matter of days – 72 hours if you really want it!!!

"Globalization is the worldwide movement toward economic, financial, trade, and communications integration. It implies the opening of local and nationalistic perspectives to a broader outlook of an interconnected and interdependent world with the mostly free transfer of capital, goods, and services across national borders."[37]

We would be doing a less-than-stellar job if we ignored the impact that globalization and technology has on customer service. After all, what this means is we can do business with almost anyone, anywhere, at any time. Naturally there are still some hurdles and limits; not all credit cards work with all online merchants; sometimes you must process through a third-party system, which has created even more opportunities in new sub-industries for companies like PayPal. And international shipping has not yet been perfected in such a way that we can have next-day air globally!

Oh! Let's not forget the super-mega-companies that do not have a physical shop presence, but trade in multiple countries have yet to get the taxation exactly right. Even in trading blocks and country unions, this is still a challenge. Take for example the EU, with multiple laws and tax structures, it would be interesting to see where this lands in a post Brexit world. There are also some barriers to entry in certain markets and some don't play fair. Sustainability remains an elusive goal and the air in many cities is not exactly fresh. But yet for all these challenges, we, as consumers, have a plethora of options, supply is everywhere, and if the corner store or local mall does not have it,

[37] BusinessDictonary.com

Richard Solomon

Alibaba, Amazon or eBay is sure to list it. If not, Google will be able to tell you where you can locate it.

A few years ago, when I was involved in an accident in my German-made SUV, the local dealer not only had ridiculous prices for replacement parts, but generally did not stock most of the parts and had extraordinarily long fulfillment times. I was able to purchase all the needed parts for the repair more quickly and cheaply by getting them online.

So available is the world to its citizens that we can easily design travel to far-off places without the help of travel agents (whatever became of the retail part of this industry?). Recently, I needed to travel to Nigeria for a project, and my office was able to effortlessly book flights that included a purposeful stop-over in Paris. I had coffee on the Champs-Élysées, visited the Arc de Triomphe, and the Eiffel Tower, all arranged from a computer located in the Southern Caribbean without ever having to speak to another person. The client sent payment via wire transfer that landed in our business account in a few days.

Our customized office stationery (we are using these less and less) is produced by an online organization called Vistaprint, here you can design almost anything in the way of business stationery and have it shipped to you at pretty decent prices. While this firm's headquarters are in Holland, customer service support might come from Jamaica, and your products could be printed in Windsor in Ontario, Canada.

There are many more examples that I can give, and I know you must have some of your own. It underscores how the world has shrunk and become so much more connected. And as the Internet has flourished in the last decade, so too have more and more apps and sites been developed as solutions to our need to be connected in this global village. It puts choice in the hand of the customer and thereby power; your competition can be coming from a completely different part of the world; **measure up or die!**

Profile of the 21st Century Customer

In addition to all that has been said before about the state of service, we must consider the customer of the 21st century. This profile has changed over the decades and clearly impacts the service landscape. Here are some quick descriptors of today's customer:

1. **Value for Money**

   Given the up-and-down fortunes of so many economies, customers the world over are very sensitive about when and for what they will part with their scarce, hard-to-come-by Dollars, Naira, Yen, Bitcoin, Euros, Pesos, Pounds, Francs, Rand, Meticals, OneCoin, Krona or whatever currency they happen to be using. They will not just hand over their cash, eWallet, plastic, or mobile pay device unless they believe they are getting real value for their money.

2. **Busy**

   Lifestyles have shifted greatly both in the East and West, with more people in a hurry and working more hours than before. More women are at work than at any other time in history, and many families only have minimal time to spend together. Between soccer practice, swimming practice, gym time, the office, grocery shopping, dinner, appointments and all the other life-necessary things people need to do, they just don't have much time. Customers don't want to wait forever for your company's systems to deliver, nor do they want to wait for things to get fixed at some distant point down the road. They want it to happen and they want it now!!!

If you or your company finds this emboldened group to be pushy, unreasonable, and overbearing, I say to you: get used to it. There is no evidence that this trend will be reversed; on the contrary, we can only expect it to increase all the more. **Measure up or die!**

3. Customization and Personalization

Not only do customers want it now, but they want it their way. The demands for customization and personalization have never been as loud as they are today. I remember sitting in a Starbucks coffee shop in Central London's Victoria Station and hearing the barista repeat a complex order that included twists, shots, and a half-skinny to the sheer delight of the waiting java lover. Philosophically, the customer is saying: "I am not a nameless, faceless, bland being who wants the same as everyone else. I am an individual; cater to me!"

Tech companies seem to be leading this effort to personalize and customize, from complex algorithms that can predict your reading interest to a flexible device called a smartphone that can be adjusted to suit your lifestyle.

4. Value versus Brand Loyalty

Brands still hold importance to customers in the 21st century, but the real loyalty is to value (and perceived value) versus the brand for its own sake. Generally, when a customer chooses a particular brand, it means they perceive some significant value to it. It may be quality, cutting-edge research, or even popularity, but it is about value in one way or another. Once customers begin to feel a loss in value, they will defect, and sometimes the defection is so great that the company cannot stand in the face of it. Netflix increased its prices a few years ago, much to the annoyance of its customer base. So great was the outcry and defection that, in 2011, they lost over 800,000 customers and approximately 27 percent of its stock value.[38] Luckily, Netflix was given a second chance by the market and has since adjusted prices. For clarity, the lucky party here is Netflix, for there are many others nipping at their heels, including Hulu and Roku. And in a classic case of social-media fueled semantic drift, couples are now meeting for "Netflix and chill."[39]

5. Test it, Try it, Sample it!

Another characteristic of today's customer is the desire to have a forehand, at-no-cost experience: Test drive a VW for 24 hours; stroll the "aisles" of the Kindle store, put titles in your cart, read samples of the books and buy them only if you like what you read. Wander into any of Apple's 499[40] (2017) retail stores, stay as long as you like, check your email on an iPad Air, call your mom on an iPhone X, or listen to music on an iPod touch.

---

[38] (Ostrow 2011)
[39] (Rose 2015)
[40] (Apple Inc. 2017a)

Richard Solomon

There is no cost to look and try, come have a taste; the CSR at Dolphin mall (Miami, Florida) food court repeatedly shouts, "orange chicken!" With small pieces of the tasty morsels on toothpicks for hungry retail warriors to sample. These organizations understand the customers' desire to try it and to sample it; they understand too that the likelihood of purchase goes up many, many times with the sample of a good product or service. These organizations know that free up-front sampling can boost sales by as much as 2,000 percent depending on the industry, the product, and other factors.[41]

The Evidence Is Overwhelming

But don't just take my word for it. After all, writers are given to the dramatic and do tend to exaggerate, don't they? Let's look at what some worldwide multi-sector research tells us about service quality, customer satisfaction, and the cost of it.

Accenture, a global management consulting, technology services, and outsourcing company, puts out an annual survey on the state of service globally. Their research shows that **64 percent of customers who switched providers did so due to poor customer service**;[42] that's 2 of every 3 people!!! Yes, customers are price-sensitive, but they still require companies to deliver with a "smile."

---

[41] (Pinsker 2014)
[42] (Accenture 2011)

Richard Solomon

The highest rates of defection are found in the retail, banking, and telecom sectors. These sectors are bleeding customers because of poor service; so bad is the bloodletting that a recent report noted that **customer churn cost** cable and telecommunications companies upwards of **US10B annually,**[43] note that this is just one sector and in the USA alone. If you think that's a bad report, look over to the other side of the Atlantic, where Pitney Bowes hailed the UK "The Customer Defection Capital of the West;" the research found that customer churn sat at a chart-topping 22 percent!!![44]

Despite all this, most companies place much greater emphasis on finding new customers than on closing the wound and stopping the hemorrhage (keeping the customers they do have). The fact is that it costs 5X more to find a new customer than to keep an old one, not to mention that repeat customers spend 33 percent more.[45]

Are you concerned about selling enough products and services to today's customers? Is ongoing performance, survival, and growth something that keeps you up at night? Do your customer-satisfaction scores tell a pretty story? Will your company be around 5-10 years down the road? All of these should be areas of concern, regardless of which industry you are in or what products and services you sell. There is no safe spot; customers can be very unforgiving, the market ruthless, and your competitors are just waiting to eat your lunch.

Are you doing enough to over-deliver to your customers? Are you tripping over yourself to do everything possible to blow customers

---

[43] (Jacada 2008)
[44] (Customer Think 2008)
[45] (LeBoeuf 2000)

Richard Solomon

away with **signature** service? If you cannot say a loud and resounding yes to these questions, roll up your sleeves and let's get to work!!!

Richard Solomon

Chapter 2

The Business Case for **Signature** *Service*

"A satisfied customer is the best business strategy of all."
— Michael LeBoeuf

"Customer service is the new marketing!" According to a American Marketing Association survey, 90 percent of consumers trust peer reviews and 70 percent trust online reviews.[46] Treat people well and they will say good things, treat them poorly and the world will know. Many leaders simply do not realize the power of service; if they did, they would be sure to make it the number one thing that their company offers. If you examine your organization's vision, mission, or values, somewhere in these words and statements you will either see the word "service," or recognize a reference to satisfying customers' needs and wants.

Business success is greatly dependent on human behavior, the behavior of the people who run the business and the people who buy from it. Businesses tend to thrive when people buy from them repeatedly and recommend them to others. These behaviors — repeat purchases and recommendations — are simply more likely when people FEEL treated well. This feeling comes from several aspects,

---

[46] (Mickiewicz 2011)

Richard Solomon

including the product itself, but the overwhelming contributor is the buying/service experience.

You are more likely to spend time with people who make you feel good or positive instead of the opposite. The same is true for customers; they are more likely to spend more time and money when you treat them well. When you treat customers positively, you are impacting a very powerful part of their brain — the middle or mammalian brain. It releases several chemicals that make it more likely for the behaviors of buying and recommending to be repeated in the future. In any type of customer interaction, a business does better by treating customers like VIPs and providing them with **signature** service.

Welcome to My Office

On a trip to Mozambique, I flew through the O.R. Tombo Airport in Johannesburg, South Africa. The 15-hour flight from New York's JFK Airport to Jo'burg was long but pleasant (more on this later), and after clearing immigration, I followed the male/female signs that lead to the restrooms. Public restrooms are generally considered necessary evils. We want to get in and out as fast as possible (well unless you are one of those people who like taking selfies in restroom mirrors, which I have always found to be a very odd practice), but I digress.

As I neared the entrance, I saw a smiling attendant who quickly said: "Welcome to my office!" Imagine my shock and surprise at hearing a bathroom attendant giving such a greeting! What do you mean "your office," I asked? He said, "this is my office, I keep it clean for you." Needless to say, I was intrigued and had to learn more.

Richard Solomon

Tell me more about this, I simply requested, and was he too happy to share. He cheerily told me that he had a very important job at the Jo'burg Airport: *"When travelers come through the airport, tired and needing to refresh themselves, I make sure that the restrooms are clean and tidy; this helps them to have a good experience and feel better overall."*

This man (let's call him Emmanuel) gets it; he is proud of his job, despite how others may perceive the nature of his work. Emmanuel uses his role to positively impact hundreds, maybe thousands of people daily. Think about what it would be like to have people in your organization who have this kind of focus, perspective, and pride!

The Business Case

There is a voice inside of me that says: *"Richard, you don't need this section."* After all, everyone knows the importance of providing quality service to customers. But do they really? I imagine if this were actually true, then more companies and individuals would be making a bigger effort to provide the **signature** service that customers deserve. Sadly, this is not the case, as we saw in chapter 1, most organizations are lagging far behind in terms of service.

My introduction to the business world came in a high school class called Principles of Business (POB). Actually, that is not entirely correct. My initial introduction to the world of business came from the handmade local delicacies my mother sold to various grocery stores in the area where we lived. She never finished primary (grade) school, but I remember her taking great care to ensure the consistency of the

Richard Solomon

coconut fudge[47] was just right and the tamarind balls[48] had the perfect balance of sour and sweet, with a slight hint of garlic and pepper.

She handled every element of the business cycle, from marketing to accounts receivable; interestingly, with no business degree she seemed to know exactly how to make it all work. As children, we all knew that the answer from daddy would most likely be "I don't have (money);" mommy on the other hand, always seemed to find a way. Once I was old enough, I worked in the packaging "department;" it was a lonely department as I was the only employee (LOL). In fact, it was the kitchen table and I was charged with the labeling, bagging, and sealing. That was really my true introduction to the world of business.

Mr. Dominic Dos Santos was my high school POB teacher and I can remember him saying that the purpose of business is to maximize profits. Most likely, you have been told the same, for it just makes good "business sense." But doesn't it follow that happy customers returning for more and telling their friends really maximizes profits? If the profit motive is the ultimate goal of business, then customer satisfaction (or better still customer delight) must be the prime mover of that profit engine.

Let's just cut to the chase and consider the positive results of providing excellent service and the negative results of not doing so. From the list of 19 facts (infographics) below, you could pick any three or four items and almost effortlessly make the case yourself.

---

[47] A sweet delicacy made from milk, sugar, coconut milk, and other ingredients, usually served in small 2-inch-square blocks.
[48] A sweet delicacy popular in the Caribbean made from sour tamarind and sugar (salt, garlic, and pepper added as desired).

Richard Solomon

Defection due to poor customer service cost companies **$338.5** billion worldwide and **$83** billion in the US alone.

Defection due to poor customer service cost companies $338.5 billion worldwide and $83 billion in the US alone.[49] Every time a customer leaves, a company incurs various costs associated with ending that relationship, and let's not forget the costs of the lost business. Companies incur even further costs in trying to find new customers to replace the ones who have defected.

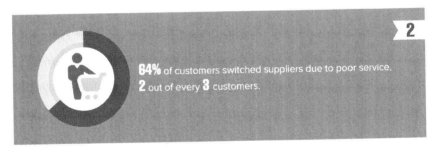

2

64% of customers switched suppliers due to poor service. **2** out of every **3** customers.

64 percent of customers switched suppliers in at least one industry due to poor service.[50] The top reason people switch is simply poor service, with 2 out of every 3 customers who leave a company doing so due to a service issue.

---

[49] (Genesys 2009)
[50] (American Express 2010)

Richard Solomon

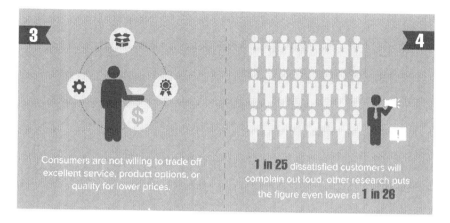

"Consumers are not willing to trade off excellent service, product options, or quality for lower prices."[51] Of course, price is important, and people are ever more careful when it comes to getting value for their money, but not at the expense of high-quality service.

1 in 25 dissatisfied customers will complain out loud, other research puts the figure even lower at 1 in 26[52]; the others will complain with their feet by taking their business elsewhere. This is a dangerous matter simply because, unless you go digging for the details, not only are they taking their business elsewhere, they are also taking information on why they left, with you none the wiser.

---

[51] (American Express 2010)
[52](CSM 2016)

Richard Solomon

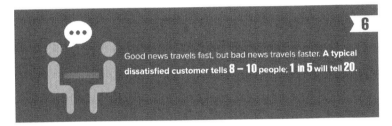

Between 44-85 percent of customers are willing to pay 5-25 percent more for a better service experience.[53]

Good news travels fast, but bad news travels faster. "A typical dissatisfied customer tells **8 – 10** people; **1 in 5 will tell 20.**"[54] We cannot take for granted the power of word-of-mouth; people are more likely to believe their friends and family than what you pay dearly to say about your brand.

Social media is the number 1 Internet activity, and 42 percent of customers will tell their friends about a good service experience and 53 percent about a bad one.[55] Social media is fast becoming the new word-of-mouth, and word spreads at the speed of a gigahertz.

---

[53] (Burke 2015)
[54] (LeBoeuf 2000)
[55] (American Express 2012)

Richard Solomon

42% of customers will tell their friends about a good service experience and 53% about a bad one they had on social media.

• Failure to respond to social media channels leads to a 15% increase in churn.
• Engaging with and responding to customer requests on social media can result in them spending 20-40% more.

Failure to respond to social media channels leads to a 15 percent increase in churn rate,[56] but engaging with and responding to customer requests on social media can result in them spending 20-40 percent more.[57]

A Google search for Customer "Complaint webpage" yielded 78.5M results in early 2018.

A Google search for "Customer Complaint webpages" yielded 78.5M results in early-2018.

---

[56] (Gartner 2012)
[57] (Barry et al. 2011)

Richard Solomon

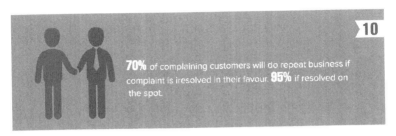

"70 percent of complaining customers will do business with you again if you resolve the complaint in their favor. If you resolve it on the spot, 95 percent will do business with you again."[58]

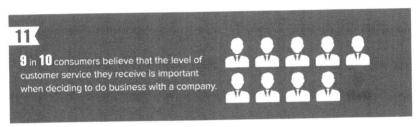

"Nine in ten consumers (90 percent) believe that the level of customer service they receive is important when deciding to do business with a company."[59]

---

[58] (LeBoeuf 2000)
[59] (American Express 2010)

Richard Solomon

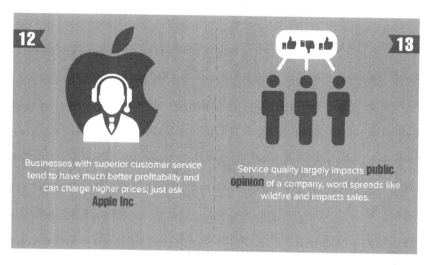

Businesses with superior customer service tend to have much better profitability and can charge higher prices; just ask **Apple Inc**

Service quality largely impacts **public opinion** of a company, word spreads like wildfire and impacts sales.

Businesses with superior customer service tend to have much better profitability and can charge higher prices; just ask Apple Inc.!!! Not only is Apple a leader in service and able to charge premium prices, they continue to be one of the world's most admired companies.[60]

Service quality largely impacts public opinion of a company, word spreads like wildfire and impacts sales. Amazon.com is a perfect example of this with their review system, which allows customers to give their honest and unfiltered opinion of products and service to all would-be buyers.

---

[60] (Colvin 2017)

Repeat customers spend on average **33%** more than new customers.

"Repeat customers spend on average 33 percent more than new customers.[61] How exciting is that?! The more repeat customers you have, the more they will likely spend with you.

Only **5%** of customers report that companies exceed their service expectations.

Only 5 percent of customers report that companies exceed their (service) expectations.

74% of customers have spent more with companies that they have positive service histories with.

More and more customers believe that businesses are paying less attention to providing good customer service.

74 percent of customers have spent more with companies that they have positive service histories with.

---

[61] (Nasir 2015)

Richard Solomon

More customers believe that businesses are paying less attention to providing good customer service.[62]

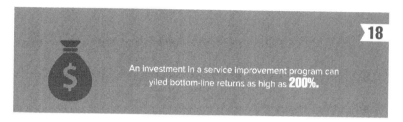

"If a company spends $1 million on a service program, it can receive $2 million in bottom-line benefits (100 percent return). For banks, return on service is as high as 170 percent and as high as 200 percent in the retail field."[63] Investing in service improvement is a sure thing, the return on investment is guaranteed.

According to the Touch Agency, over 1 million people view tweets about customer service each week – 80 percent of which are negative.[64]

---

[62] (American Express 2014)
[63] (Tschohl 2011)
[64] (Help Scout 2018)

Richard Solomon

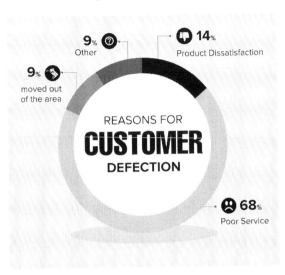

Infographic 24: Reasons for Customer Defection[65]

Is the Case Made?

So there you have it — 19 clear facts (plus 1) that make the case for **signature** service, and what a picture it paints! I could have easily written a page or four about each of these points, adding more stuff than you care to read. But that is not what this book is about; it is about what you, your people, your company can do to greatly improve the service quality that you deliver to your customers. Here is what these facts are saying in summary: Pay attention to your customers and serve them in the way they want, and they will reward you for it. If you do the opposite, you do so at your own risk!

If somewhere inside you still have doubts about the importance of customer service to a company, then I suggest you look around your own circles, even your company, to find factors that make the case. Don't force it, just look, or better yet, call up a few customers and ask

---

[65] (Accenture 2011)

Richard Solomon

their opinion, ask your friends and family, and **wait for it...!** Depending on where you look and whom you ask, you will find a variety of stories. What will be consistent is that most customers are not happy with what passes for service and they would be glad to pay more to companies that meet their expectations. Why an organization would not do all they could to deliver **signature** service is a question that we all ask.

As a customer yourself, you can recall times that you have walked away from a transaction, ended a business relationship, or bought less than you intended because of the poor quality of service. I figure your experiences are enough to make the case.

Most Organizations Are Completely Confused

Bain and Company is a global consulting firm headquartered in Boston, Massachusetts with 54 offices in 34 countries. They are one of what is known as the Big Three (consulting firms), the others are McKinsey & Co., and The Boston Consulting Group (of BCG Matrix fame). In their seminal work called "Closing the Delivery Gap," Bain conducted research on 362 companies and their customers. The research team included Frederich Reichheld, who is the creator of the Net Promoter System of management. Amazingly, among other things, the research found that, while 80 percent of companies believed they were giving their customers a "superior experience," only 8 percent of their customers agreed as seen in the graphic below (infographic 25).[66]

---

[66] (Allen et al. 2005)

Richard Solomon

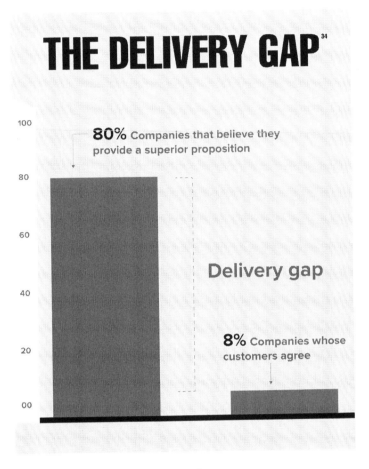

Infographic 25

This is an astounding gap; why would such a disparity exist between what companies believe and what their customers know? Notice I did not say what companies know, or what customers believe. Knowing is for the customers; they are the **only ones** who truly *know* what they want and what will give them the best experience. Bain puts forward two central reasons for this gap. The **first** is what they call "the paradox of business." They noted that most growth initiatives damage the customer franchise; efforts to increase revenue lead to

Richard Solomon

increased fees and the alienating of core customer groups. **Secondly**, efforts to grow the customer base can also be damaging, as this can distract management from core customers who are already there (effectively taking them for granted).

The research further went on to reveal that only half of management teams design their products and services to meet the needs of customers. Only 30 percent organize the functions of the company to deliver superior customer experiences, with only a similar amount maintaining effective customer feedback loops.[67]

It is astounding that so many organizations are confused about what their customers truly experience and want! Misguided about what is really valuable to the customer, daily focusing on failing products, annoying processes, and cumbersome systems that do nothing but drive space between the brand and its would-be fans.

In my experience, too many companies focus on the bottom-line, profit-per-transaction, throughput volumes, KPIs, and similar metrics. These are all important, but not when their focus is misaligned to what the customer truly values. You do have a business to run and setting goals and keeping track is without a doubt necessary. But if your company falls into the 50 percent of companies that do not properly design products and services to meet the needs of customers, or the 70 percent that are not organizing functions to deliver a superior experience, the sad truth is that all the other foci and effort is wasted energy and resources.

---

[67] (Allen et al. 2005)

Richard Solomon

The Numbers Don't Lie

The more I think about it, the more I see mounting evidence of the impact of service on the financial returns of organizations. Had you invested one thousand dollars (US) in each of the following "service organizations" back in January 2008, Table 3 below shows what each stocks' worth would be in January 2018. [68]

---

[68] (Nasdaq 2018)

Richard Solomon

COMPANY (NASDAQ SYMBOL)	INDUSTRY	STOCK PRICE JAN. 2008	STOCK PRICE JAN. 2018	VALUE OF $1K INVESTMENT @ JAN. 2018
amazon	E-comm.	82.18	1273.39	$15506.45
THE HOME DEPOT	Hardware	25.10	195.50	$7788.85
Apple	Technology	25.36	176.36	$6954.26
Southwest	Aviation	11.77	65.21	$5540.36
jetBlue	Aviation	4.83	22.43	$4643.89
Disney	Various	30.50	111.32	$3649.84
UNITED	Aviation	32.07	76.74	$2392.89
American Airlines	Aviation	23.95	56.56	$2361.59
Walmart	Consumer Goods	47.98	101.39	$2113.17
BEST BUY	Consumer Electronics	44.64	71.79	$1608.20

Table 3

Richard Solomon

We know that correlation does not prove causation, and therefore we cannot simply conclude that if a company gives great service, they will enjoy excellent financial returns. We know that stock prices are affected by much more than the quality of service that the company delivers. The general state of the economy, actions of executives, growth in adjacent industries, aggressiveness of competitors, societal shifts and geopolitics can all impact how well a company does on the stock exchange. Additionally, the market can be fickle and investors are given to panic, notwithstanding the fact that the market always rises.

Every share price on our table has increased, however it's hard to miss that the return on investment (ROI) leaders are also some of the best service leaders as well. The converse is true for laggards like Walmart, United and American Airlines, they too have increased in value but at a much slower rate than the service giants. Best Buy may be an outlier here, while their service is far from stellar, its fortunes have certainly been negatively affected by the rise in e-commerce with competitors like Amazon leading the onslaught.

Another Amazing Payoff

Just in case you are still not convinced, or you harbor some doubt about the importance of service to the overall success of an organization, there is another benefit, actually a series of benefits that flow from working to develop the service quality of your organization. Unlike some other changes and improvements that may just require a stroke of the pen or a new piece of equipment, this kind of improvement requires real growth in deeper areas. One such example is the involvement of leaders, as we will see in chapter 4, leaders have

Richard Solomon

a major role to play in the service journey. Leaders must simply become better at leading people – this will positively impact service and many other areas of the business including productivity, employee engagement, and innovation.

Richard Solomon

Chapter 3

The Service Challenge – Why Is It so Difficult?

Humans are special beings because we are constantly being impacted by, and having an impact on the environment around us. Our experiences largely shape who we are, and the experiences of our fore-parents also contribute to our current state. What does all of this have to do with service, you ask? Well, unlike a tangible product, our perception of service quality is largely shaped by who we are on the inside. Our internal state influences how we see the outer world and interact with it and the people in it.

Our sense of what constitutes good service varies from culture to culture, one society to another, and one person to another. If you grew up in a society or family where people tended to be more aggressive, dismissive, sociable, gentle, or kind, you most likely would have developed coping or "comfort mechanisms" to manage yourself and succeed in those situations. They would be familiar to you and your tolerance and dexterity would be higher and more well-adapted than those of someone who had different formative experiences.

We have all seen movies where someone goes to a small restaurant run by a middle-aged person who seems too much on edge. The interaction is anything but picture-perfect, but the food is to die for.

Something about the personality of the place, the history and the patrons' sense of what good looks like makes it right for them. Think of Carla, the waitress from the sitcom Cheers; she was known for her sharp tongue, quick-cutting wit and biting sarcasm; hardly what you might call **signature** service. But in the context of the show and given the characters, her way was a crucial component of the bar's experience, as was Woody's dim mind.

The examples described above are special, and they do not represent the norm; in the average service situation, the desire is for providers who are sharp, well-mannered, willing, and personable. But the point here is that the perception of what is "good" depends on the environment and your own experiences.

So What Is Signature Service?

Signature service is the continuous delivery of a predetermined VIP-level customer experience across all platforms, at all service points, and flash points to all customers. To be clear, let us quickly examine a few of these components:

1. **Continuous** – Not hit-or-miss or dependent on a certain person, location, time, or other variable.
2. **Predetermined** – Mapped or planned beforehand, not accidental or incidental.
3. **VIP Level** – Of the highest standard, order, and quality.
4. **All Platforms** – Found in every place that your customer interfaces with your brand.
5. **Service Points** – Predictable, recurring opportunities to serve the customer.

Richard Solomon

6. **Flash Points** – Unpredictable situations or opportunities to serve the customer.

7. **All Customers** – High-quality service for all customers even when different customer segments exist.

If you examine this definition and its components, you immediately recognize two important facts: The **first** is that you as a customer (like all customers) would be overjoyed to receive this type of service from any provider; **secondly**, delivering such service is not simple or commonplace or else more companies would be doing it.

Of the seven components above, I suspect most readers will get stuck on the VIP-level service for all customers, after all, **how could you possibly treat everyone like a VIP?** In the modern era, we have developed a type of celebrity deification where we view and treat certain people as better than others. The wealthy, super-popular entertainers, sporting heroes, and politicians all seem to effortlessly fall into the VIP class, and these people are seen as being special and different, unable to do wrong (until they do of course).

But think of it, how much of your business volume (if any) comes from these groups and any other VIP types you can identify? Isn't it fair to say that the people who really support your business year-round, the ones who keep the profits coming in, are *your true VIPs*? But if a VIP (as commonly defined) were to walk into your business place right now, they would likely be treated so much better than your everyday customer.

This is misplaced thinking. Yes, I know that it is natural for us humans to be more pleasant with and helpful to people we recognize and like, and I also know that it may not be economically feasible to

Richard Solomon

devote the level of resources (people, time, space) that you extend to a big spender to the everyday, smaller-transaction buyer. However, what we are seeking to create here is high-quality experiences at every turn, to make the service points so refined and the flash points so effortless and easy for the customer that Joe, Jane, and John Public all feel like VIPs.

Signature means that it is the kind of service that makes customers exclaim "wow!!!" I sometimes like to call it "tripping-over-themselves-service." A group of people so bent on giving customers a VIP experience that they run and jump to make it happen. To you, customers are not a bother or an inconvenience; in fact, they are exactly the opposite. They are the main reason you open the doors daily. And so all systems, processes, approaches, products, and services are designed with the customer in mind. In this situation, the customer is not a King; the customer is truly an Emperor![69]

You will know **signature** service when you see it, in the same way you will know when it's painfully absent. Don't get me wrong, I am not for one moment suggesting that organizations should be set up to slave after customers' every whim and fancy, after all people can be unreasonable, and this is not sustainable. But **signature** service says: "I am super happy you came to us with your business and we are going to exceed your expectations, even if we have to bend and jump to do it. We see you as a VIP and are willing to treat you like one at every interaction."

---

[69] *A King rules over his Kingdom (an independent state), an Emperor rules over his empire, which is a group of countries.*

Richard Solomon

The company does not play Russian roulette with service delivery; the customer does not have to go to that special department, branch, or person to get **signature** service. Many of us have been there, preferring to go to or speak with that one person who in the past has and will in the future deliver **signature** service. This means that either you have had bad experiences with others in the same company, or you just don't trust that they will do as good a job.

Why should a customer have to postpone their interaction with your company for fear of poor service? Why should they have to call again because the one super service hero is not available? Why should they have to visit a more distant location just to see "THE ONE?" Why should they have to wait a day for a response on social media and then be directed back to the same slow company systems? Not only does it annoy and throw off plans, it can potentially lose or reduce business for the company and **frankly nobody wins – well except the competition.**

Signature service is consistent, customers don't guess, they don't worry, they don't ask for "THE ONE," they don't leave disappointed. They make contact and feel confident that their matters will be dealt with in a speedy, engaged, and professional manner. **Signature** service is consistent and continuous; it does not depend on the moods of employees nor their goodwill to "help us out." Don't you just hate it when a service provider, speaks or behaves like they are doing you a favor by "helping you out?" I know in some cultures, the phrase "let me help you out" is taken as positive. But some service providers sadly don't even know better; they honestly think that it is a good thing that they are trying to do the customer a "favor." This mentality of doing the customer favors flies in the face of true **signature** service. Sitting at the base of the **signature** service strategy is an understanding that the customers are actually helping you out by spending their money with your organization!

The 3Ps of Signature Service (the major determinants)

Delighting customers who have varying experiences, education levels, problems and a long list of other characteristics can be daunting. The customer experience from the organization's side is largely determined by three key factors: **Products, processes, and people**. We will look at the customer experience in greater detail in chapter 9, but for now, let's examine these three key factors to answer the question about why service delivery is so hard.

1. Product

The word product comes from the Latin *productum* meaning "thing." It can be defined as the totality of goods and services produced by an organization. It is the primary "thing(s)" that the organization produces to sell to its customers and in some cases - the product *is* a service. Very often, the product is the starting place, an idea in someone's head that will fill a gap or meet a need. Products are central to business success and deserve significant attention, most organizations therefore place a great deal of focus on the products they make and/or sell. Plant, machinery, systems, design, raw materials, labor are usually top-of-mind as organizations are configured, built, outfitted, and developed. Leaders usually do all they can to get the product right, and even though there are sometimes

Richard Solomon

catastrophic failures, it is safe to say that, of the three, products usually get the highest priority.

2. Processes

A process is a set of systemic actions directed to some output or end-result, and it is derived from the Latin *processus* meaning "a moving forward." Most organizations have multitudes of processes, but for our purposes we will quickly examine three types. The **first** are the ones used to produce the product (or service) that the organization sells; these include research and development, production, and quality control. When it comes to quality, most organizations have spent a lot of money developing systems to ensure consistency of output.

The **second** are the ones used to manage the customer's experience in the process of selling and providing related support services. Obviously these include service delivery, marketing, sales, and delivery. The **third** set of processes are the people processes, those that are used to manage the human capital or human resources of the organization.

3. People

I choose to separate the people from the processes that lead and manage people because people are the secret ingredient in any organization. People impact and influence the first two (product and process) and, in large measure, determine the success or failure of an organization. The people component is the most difficult to manage in any project, firm, or organization, and because few managers possess true leadership skills naturally, and even fewer still have spent any

Richard Solomon

significant time developing these skills, this problem is always compounded.

You want to get your service right; you want your organization to be a shining star, a bright example. You want your customers to be happy, to be promoters, you want them to recommend you and your products, and these are worthy goals. I can say without any fear of contradiction that, if you do not get the people part correct, your service will always be poor or, at best, average.

The True Difficulty

The people component is the real difficulty in the service formula. At every level of the organization, if the people component is not right, then the service will be wrong. Let's quickly consider a few examples:

1. On the front line, customers are not having a pleasant experience – **people** man the front lines.
2. Systems are too complicated and tend to frustrate customers – **people** designed and operate the systems.
3. Products fail too early, causing bad publicity and reduced return business – **people** designed the products, manage their production, and the quality-assurance systems.
4. Policies seem designed to only protect the business from the 3 percent of customers who tend be dishonest in their claims (effectively punishing the 97 percent) – **people** enact and uphold the policies.
5. Resources are scantily invested on the human side of the business, but generously on the systems and technology sides – **people** make these resource-allocation decisions.

Richard Solomon

6. Employees are not engaged and tend to drone though their day – **people** choose and lead employees.

7. Executives seem mainly concerned about the bottom line – executives are **people.**

8. The customer experience seems not to have a strategic position in the C Suite – such decisions and positioning are executed by **people.**

9. Customer defection is higher than you think it should be – customers leave mainly for poor service, which is delivered by **people.**

10. Your Net Promoter Score is lower than your major competitors' – there is some thing or some things that **people** are doing or not that is influencing this.

I am not saying that the people factor is the only element you need to pay attention to, far from it. What I am saying, however, is that the biggest challenges and opportunities organizations face in delivering **signature** service are people-related. The organization is built by, operated by, and improved by people, and nothing happens unless people move. This is so much truer in the service domain.

There is Hope

Hope is that quintessential human catalyst, that thing that keeps us trying, moving ahead despite the tremendous odds we sometimes face. It is represented in the student who has failed a course yet again and refuses to give up – hope. The rookie pitcher who can't seem to put the ball directly over the plate twice in a row, but keeps trying – hope. The amateur basketball player who has been on the court for hours, doing yet another jump shot – hope. It is the parent who

Richard Solomon

refuses to give up on a wayward teenager – hope. The married couple that agrees to try again and again despite hurts and pains – hope. This amazing thing called hope keeps us going against all odds.

Henry Ford had hope and refused to quit even after his first two automobile companies failed. Michael Jordan was cut from his high school basketball team, went home, locked himself in his room and cried. But he had hope – and now he has six NBA championship rings to go with all that hope. Oprah Winfrey was demoted from her job as a news anchor because she "wasn't fit for television!" Steve Jobs was unceremoniously removed from the company he started; but went on to buy Pixar and build it into the behemoth that gave us such hits as *Cars, Up* and *Toy Story* - hope. He returned to Apple and built it into the largest company in the world by market capitalization (over 878B - 2017); hope certainly turned into a huge success for Jobs. At his death, Jobs was the single-largest shareholder of the Disney corporation, according to *Time* magazine.[70]

Have you ever written or said something, looked back on it and said "hmmmmm?" That is how I feel about this introduction to this section; somehow it feels a little personal development/motivational(ish). But you know what? I honestly believe that people, like organizations, can change. My hope is based on more than just stories of famous people; it is based on years of work with thousands of individuals and firms in many countries that have changed, ranging from the little tweaks to huge revamps. It is also based on my own journey of change, self-improvement, and

---

[70] (Greelish 2013)

Richard Solomon

growth and the multiple journeys of individuals and organizations I am fortunate enough to have been a part of or known.

Hope – I start with hope because I know, for some of you, this service journey might seem hopeless. Maybe you have tried to plug one hole or fix some problem only to have five more show up the next morning. Maybe you have done your best to keep customers from defecting, but the rate remains too high. Maybe your company has spent money on hiring, training, and retraining staff, but still falls short of where you need to be. Maybe the customer complaints department is asking for more people, which means they have too many complaints. Maybe you are an executive who understands the value of service, but you cannot convince the rest of your executive colleagues to put the needed resources into delivering the right service experience. I know how difficult this can be; I have coached many leaders dealing with similar problems.

But I know there is hope; it starts with the strategies in this book. This is a formula and road map providing the pieces you need and the steps you need to take. Not only have mega-companies used them, but I have helped many organizations go from one step to the other and seen real improvement.

Organizations are systemic in nature, they are connected up, down, and across in such a way that, when you adjust one component, it impacts others. But it *is* because they are systemic; we can make changes like the ones I am suggesting here. Systems have inputs, throughputs, and outputs, and they operate within an environment context. The adjustment of any of these components creates a change that can usually be seen in particular outputs — and possibly elsewhere.

The people component shines a big ray of hope for improvement because people can change or they can be changed. In case you passed over that last line, let me repeat; people can change or they can be changed, we won't sacrifice the good of the whole for the one. Service to the customer is the number one reason your company opens the doors, it is the most important strategy the organization could ever employ. It follows that you should pull out all the stops (including human ones) to create and deliver **signature** service to your valuable customers.

What we will do in this text is walk step-by-step together and examine how you can make adjustments to create the **signature** service you want to deliver, and your customers deserve. Read on!

Richard Solomon

Chapter 4

Leaders Go First

The Role of leadership

The Costa Concordia ran aground off the coast of Italy in early January 2012, and 32 souls perished. Captain Schettino was already on land, while many of his passengers were fighting for their lives and dying within the wreck. He tried to explain away his actions, including blaming his helmsman, Jacob Bin. Schettino was brought to book and after a 19-month trial was sentenced to 16 years in prison. He was separately punished for causing the wreck, manslaughter, and abandoning his crew.[71]

Captain Chesley Burnett "Sully" Sullenberger III was in command of US Airways flight 1549, just eight days before his 58th birthday on January 15, 2009. His Airbus A320 hit a flock of Canadian Geese somewhere over New York City, disabling both GE engines. No one had ever trained for this, and there were no simulations. In those early seconds of this pending disaster, Captain Sully made a fateful decision. Against the advice of the control tower, he decided not to try for a return to La Guardia Airport, nor an emergency landing at JFK or Teterboro. Instead, he took control of the aircraft, saying "my plane!" to his co-pilot and informing the tower that they would be

---

[71] (ABC News 2015)

Richard Solomon

landing in the Hudson River. His only communication to the passengers was: "This is the captain — brace for impact!"[72]

Although it took the NTSB[73] 15 months to declare that Captain Sully made the right decision, we all instinctively believed that his decisions and the actions of the crew were perfect given the circumstances. Together, they gave us what is now commonly known as the "Miracle on the Hudson." Every one of the 155 souls on board survived, and there were no serious injuries; it was and still is the only successful commercial flight landing on the Hudson River.

"Everything rises and falls on leadership."[74] If a cruise ship runs aground, you don't blame the helmsman; no one in their right mind would hold him or her responsible. Instead we all look to the captain. Sure, there may have been extenuating circumstances or a "complex disaster" as in the case of the Concordia, and maybe he or she could not have known of the existence of the particular challenges beforehand. But guess what? We still look to the captain; after all, this is his ship and he has all of the passengers' lives in his hands; ultimately, he is responsible. The buck stops there!

In like manner, Captain Sully is a hero, for he did what he thought was right and, even though it was not by the book, he was in charge, it was his airplane, and he was responsible. The buck stopped with him!

Sitting at the top, leaders can act as limiting forces, curbing the potential of the organization to do great things, or they can be the exact opposite — booster rockets that truly propel the organization

---

[72] (Sullenberger and Zaslow 2009)
[73] National Transport Safety Board
[74] (Maxwell 2007)

Richard Solomon

into the stratosphere. The truth of the matter is it is very hard for the organization to grow past the leader when the leader is limited and limiting. They erect invisible barriers that hold the people, the progress, and the growth process back. A leader with a big vision for the future can and often does create the future. Jobs and his companies directly revolutionized several industries, including music, personal computing, movie animation, and mobile phones.

So it is in the domain of service; if an organization is to provide **Signature** Service, then it must have leaders who make this both a strategic and operational priority. It cannot be an afterthought or something that is done occasionally; it must remain the focus — the bull's eye, the reason that everyone gets up and comes to the office every day. Make no mistake; a company or department whose most-senior leaders do not have this focus cannot deliver **signature** service consistently. This is not optional. In the war to deliver **signature** service, leaders, you take point!

Remember leaders are ultimately in charge of such critical factors as policy, resource allocation, and decision-making at varying levels. Often when a customer is seeking some kind of redress because they believe they have been wronged, they are met with the "I am sorry, but that's outside our policy" response. That policy is enacted and upheld by leadership.

SPL Did It Right from the Start

A few years ago, a retail start-up contacted me to help them get their service culture right from the start. David, the CEO who had had a long and successful career in sales with a Fortune 100 company, was clear: he wanted service to be the big draw for customers, since service was what they were actually selling. Being in the retail pharmacy business, there were many competitors, and he knew that if they provided "WOW [75] service consistently," it would give them the winning edge they wanted.

And they did it too. The recruitment process was designed with service in mind – seeking out persons with customer-friendly attitudes; the gondola shelving was below eye level so that associates could see customers across the store and respond to them quickly. Every staff member spent days in customer service training long before one pill was ever sold; all managers and executives were trained in managing for WOW service before one dollar was made! They were well on their way, and let me tell you, did they ever make a huge impact; the service was WOW for sure! I visited many times in those early days to see how things were going. I talked to customers to get their take and people agreed — this company was doing something special, something different from many of their competitors.

From the associate who would notice from the end of the aisle that you had too many items in your hands to shop comfortably and rush you a mini cart; to the supervisor who called up a competitor to find you a particular product because they were out of stock and just wanted to make the customer happy even if it meant the *loss* of *that* sale. Then there was the pregnant customer who had a hankering for buttered popcorn; purchased a pack and expressed that she could not wait to get home and prepare it, and the eagle-eyed associate who offered to take the package to the staff kitchen, and pop it in the

---

[75] WOW was their own brand of Signature Service

Richard Solomon

microwave so that the customer could enjoy it right away, much to the delight of the expectant mother. WOW!!!

Leadership makes all the difference, and this great start could not have happened had the CEO not latched onto a vision and held firm to it. He was prepared to do what was needed to make wow service what the organization was about.

The Chance of Being Struck by Lightning Twice

It is not good enough to provide excellent service once in a while, that would mean that the customer would have to play Russian Roulette, not being sure if the service would be great today, at this outlet, with this CSR, or so bad that they wonder if they were in the right organization. Service should not be a lottery. Do you know that you stand a better chance of being struck by lightning twice than winning most lotteries? And this is how some organizations are when it comes to service delivery — haphazard, erratic, and inconsistent. Some days it's great and others well... customers hope for the best, but expect much less.

A bank that I have done business with for years immediately comes to mind. Private Banking customers are entitled to certain privileges, which include no lines, having one person conduct all your transactions, sitting in a private office versus standing in the banking hall, and being able to get that same quick, friendly "I know you" service at any branch throughout the network. But here is where the service loses consistency. If I go to my home branch, then all goes well, the service is usually efficient and friendly. However, at times I would be in another area with a transaction to do. Instead of

Richard Solomon

scrambling to get to my home branch before closing time (2 p.m. is way too early by the way – bankers' hours make no sense to customers), I would just TRY to get the transactions done at whichever branch happened to be nearest.

Well, good luck with that, as I might as well have played the lottery. In each case, I was met with service, body language, and words that seemed to say some or all of the following:

- *Is this your home branch (why should it matter)?*
- *Did someone say you were coming (appointments are not required)?*
- *Why are you here (I am a customer!!!!)?*
- *Do we know you (No you know my money!!!)?*
- *Please wait until someone is available (20 minutes - what the firetruck!!!???)*

This should never happen, especially when the bank sold the same service, network-wide as a draw to get my business. On one of these ill-advised efforts, I was asked by one CSR "Sir, who are you?" Not "what was my name" or "may I please have your name," but *"who are you?"* I was truly annoyed by the question, as I had already given my name; I curtly and sarcastically responded, *"oh I am nobody special, just a customer!"* Her annoyance was a bit difficult to hide, and I quickly asked for the branch manager who instantly recognized me and called me into her office to find out what was the problem. This service pro quickly apologized for the wait and the behavior of the CSR; had me wait in her office while someone attended to my transactions, and someone else brought the coffee.

Richard Solomon

But why should it be this way? Why should a customer have to complain, speak in a different language (sarcasm), ask for the manager, or be recognized in order to get the service quality that the bank promised in the first place?

I can tell you why; it is because no one had thought through what it really means to give **signature** service at this bank. The leadership either has not built this into the systems and processes, or has not ensured that people have been trained and that training is not left as a standalone event. It could be that the measurement and oversight of service delivery is weak.

Customers should not have to win the lottery to get **signature** service from your organization on a consistent basis. Make it "just the way you do business."

Leaders and Strategy

In late 2007, the tenuous merger between Sprint and Nextel had a big question mark looming over it. At his first operational meeting with senior managers in January 2008, CEO Danny Hesse asked which of the top three executives was responsible for appeasing disgruntled customers. No hands went up! Sprint identified customer services as its biggest problem but did not have one single executive accountable.[76]

If you want your service to stand out, there are two strategic leadership moves that must be made:

---

[76] (Holson 2008)

Richard Solomon

1. The organization must articulate a strategy that supports the service vision.

2. Someone in the C-suite must be directly responsible and held accountable.

Don't Forget the Middle

Middle managers have more contact with the broader organizational base than the C-suite. These critical people are linking pins and need to be enrolled in the strategy from the start. While the top executives have the power, the middle has the reach and most strategies are doomed to failure if they are not involved.

On Strategy Making

Essentially, a company's strategy involves the competitive moves and approaches management will employ to grow the business, gain and satisfy customers, compete successfully, and hit performance targets.[77]

Much has been written on the topic of strategy, definitions abound, and models are in abundant supply. Without belaboring the point, here is what we must note: If service is to stand out and truly provide a competitive advantage, then the service intent should permeate all levels of strategy.

1. **Corporate Strategy** – Looks at the whole, and a key question here is: **What business are we really in?** The only answer should be "we are in the service business."

---

[77] (Thompson and Thompson 2012)

Richard Solomon

2. **Business Unit Strategy** – These are the battle plans used to fight the competition in the industry. A key question is: **How will we position ourselves vis-a-vis our competition regarding service delivery?**

3. **Functional Strategy** – The value-added activities that management chooses for the business. A key question is: **Which activities will add the most value for our customers?**

If you believe that service is truly critical to your company's success, but there is no strategy that speaks to service, then clearly it's not as important (to the company) as you believe.

Signature Service is a Strategic Weapon

I know, you cannot simply whittle business strategy down to serving the customer well; after all, there are such complicated issues and barriers to entry, price elasticity of demand, market saturation, operational efficiencies, and human capital management. I am not suggesting for a minute that we ignore all that important stuff, but focusing on all those and ignoring or only paying lip service to the customer is downright senseless. Yet, few organizations truly make customers feel so special that they want to return.

One Christmas, my family and I took a short Bahamas cruise as part of our end-of-year vacation. I had tried for years to get the rest of the clan to agree to a cruise and finally there was unanimity; my immediate family is comprised of all women, I am always outnumbered and very rarely feel the need to issue executive orders (they wouldn't take me seriously anyway).

Richard Solomon

The Royal Caribbean (RC) Majesty of the Seas crew were super nice. Estaban, who was responsible for our cabin, really made us feel special. Everyone was great, and I cannot help but observe service interactions around me and RC hit all the right notes. There was the time that we were late for some meal, just getting to that restaurant as they were about to close. Obviously, the crew needed to clean up and reset the tables so there had to be a closing time, but you know what? The smiling attendant seemed happy to remove the velvet cordon rope and, with a hint of mischievousness, he said, it's ok but just this once. He was not too concerned about how letting in a few more guests would mess up their schedule and workflow; he was obviously more concerned about being hospitable to his guests. We will be back; once I am not outvoted.

Service like that is not accidental, because people don't just do it well because you wish it, and systems and processes don't just work in concert to create a delightful customer experience. They happen because leaders are on the job; leaders go first!

Articulating a Signature Service Vision

One of the commonalities I have found with **signature** service companies is that they all have a very clear vision, which points to providing that kind of service. It is often one of the first places I start with my own clients' leaders. What is your vision for this company in terms of service – what do you care about enough to make happen? Here are a few examples of service visions/mission:

Richard Solomon

1. **Amazon.com**: *"Our number one goal is to be the earth's most customer-centered company."*[78] You can't make it much clearer than this.

2. **Disney**: *"To make people happy."*[79] Badly treated customers are not happy nor do they usually return for very long.

3. **Southwest Airlines**: *"Dedication to the highest quality of Customer Service delivered with a sense of warmth, friendliness, individual pride and Company Spirit."*[80] They interestingly added a few key interpersonal components.

4. **Zappos**: *"Deliver wow through service."*[81] This is actually the first of ten Zappos values that point to amazing customers through service delivery.

5. **Ritz Carlton**: *"Ladies and gentlemen serving ladies and gentlemen"*[82] Ladies and gentlemen behave in a particular manner and deserve nothing less than excellence.

Whether you call it vision, mantra, tagline, or some other catchy name, your company needs to have a statement that has real meaning and serves to guide people, align resources, design processes, guide behavior, and organize systems.

The vision is a point of alignment for all the efforts and resources of the organization, a beacon or lighthouse. Imagine everyone in the company having line-of-sight to a **common end-result**. A good

---

[78] (Amazon 2018)
[79] (Rasmus 2012)
[80] (Southwest Airlines 2018b)
[81] (Zappos.com 2018)
[82] (The Ritz-Carlton 2017)

Richard Solomon

vision leads to competitive advantage and acts as a fundamental impetus in empowering people to serve customers.

The word "vision" as it is used here is not meant to conjure images of management-developed statements of the abstract and far-fetched, nor is it about smart-sounding marketing-speak that can be seen on promo materials and hanging in lobbies. Hang it in the lobby if you will, use it for promos if you like, but ensure it represents a real, identifiable future state that all processes, efforts, people, decisions, and resources can be aligned to. One that people can hang their hopes on and know every day why they are coming to work. They need to know the why, not just the how.

On Building a Vision

To win the devotion of customers, leaders must build an organization worthy of devotion. You cannot win the hearts (and minds) of customers unless your own heart and mind is in the game. Yet far too many organizations/leaders lack that essential zeal. They suffer what Charlotte Beers (Chairman Emeritus of Ogilvy & Mather) calls "heart failure." Some of the symptoms of this disease include:

1. *Key managers have different versions of the company's strategy, mission or vision.*

2. *Employees don't know what the company stands for.*

3. *Recognition, promotions, and everyday actions show a bias against mavericks and risk-takers.*

Richard Solomon

4. *Communications within and outside the organization are marked by dry, dull, and sober language.*

5. *Political in-fighting and fiefdoms prevail.*

6. *Customer and employee feedback reveals a gap between the company's intentions and constituents' perceptions.*[83]

The vision is a description of your company's ideal future state. It is not a pipedream or some fantasy; instead it captures the highest aspirations of the business. There are many processes a company can use to create a vision. A small team of executives can do it; input can be gathered from the wider body corporate, with cross-functional teamwork, to create the actual statement. It can be part of the strategic planning process, founders can articulate it, and so on.

Regardless how you come up with it, leaders are the custodians of the vision and must ensure that the organization is designed and set up to make it a reality. As the external environment shifts, so too does its internal design, efforts, and processes. But the vision generally stays constant over the long term, and it stands as a lighthouse beckoning everyone in its direction.

Go after profit for sure, but you need to also ensure that people are going after purpose. If your organization can articulate this purpose in a manner that speaks to creating something bigger than itself, and if it

---

[83] (Hesselbein and Cohen 1999)

Richard Solomon

can imbed the purpose (the why) in all that the organization does and its product, processes, and people, you have a winner![84]

Run, strive, shoot, lunge; work hard and smart to make it happen. But the leader must put his money where his mouth is and support the vision wholeheartedly. Have a heart for the organization and its vision and do what you must to ensure that organizational leaders do not suffer heart failure and are committed to making the vision a reality.

Turning the Organization on Its Head

I honestly believe that the structure of organizations is upside down from a customer service perspective. If I had my way, the very structure of organizations would look like the figure below, with the customers at the top and the CEO (and other managers) closer the bottom in servant leadership positions.

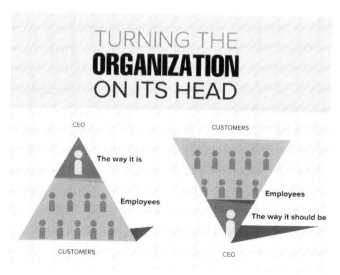

Infographic 26

---

[84] (Hakimi 2015)

Richard Solomon

The servant leader is a servant first; he understands that serving others enables them to do their best work. He does not feel any less of a leader because of the servant position. On the contrary, she realizes that her greatest accomplishment is **firstly** being a futurist that holds a very clear vision of what the organization should and could be. **Secondly**, she is a facilitator who enables people to execute the company's strategy with excellence. Servant leaders know that their job is to support others in doing their best work; they lead by example in giving excellent service to *their* customers (staff and other leaders) and have the unwavering resolve to treat others with respect and dignity.

Servant leaders are in no way weak; in fact, they are usually judged by history to be giants among women and men. Think of names like Yeshua the Christ, Gandhi, and Mandela; these are all examples of servant leaders who enabled others and facilitated transformations through servanthood.

Differentiation

Differentiation is a term more commonly used in marketing, but I think it fits in nicely here. **Here is a great opportunity for your company**: Because poor service is so much the norm, an organization offering excellent service immediately stands out positively. **Signature** service will make your company stand head and shoulders above the competition. If what you offer in terms of the product itself won't set you apart, **signature** service certainly will.

I previously gave several examples of categories that were crowded with multiple competitors. Very few organizations have the good fortune of being the only. Thinking about it, monopoly status does not always ensure business success or strong growth. Competition can be a useful force for industry development. In this connected world where efficiency, creativity, and disruption are the names of the game, your company and its products are likely to be among a group of others battling for the customers' attention and financial resources. The marketplace continues to be crowded, but service continues to be a key differentiator, with those giving excellent service consistently finding themselves alone (or with few true companions) in their respective product categories.

Value-Addition

Maybe you have a great product or service, or maybe it's not so great and can get lost in the crowd of others. When you add **signature** service to this product or service, you instantly augment it to the delight of your customers. The value addition is instant and worth its weight in gold. Daily I watch companies competing on price. With all the price wars and low-cost ads plastered everywhere, you would think that this is the top reason why people buy. Naturally, everyone wants a good deal, but remember what we saw earlier in chapter 2 — customers are willing to pay more when the service quality is higher.

Obviously, good business practice demands that a company is clear about whom they are pitching their product to. Different customer groups have varying levels of disposable income, and a company's focus can make a world of difference in terms of their revenue and profits. But regardless of how rich your market segment is (or is not), all customers are more willing to return when they are well-served. This is a truism for the rich and poor, for the East and West, for the young and mature.

Richard Solomon

Not Easily Duplicated

As a strategic weapon, **signature** service can blow away (not to mention confuse) your competition. But it is not an easy or a simple thing to do, because to do it you have to do so many others things well. And most business leaders don't have the stick-to-it-iveness (yep this one is a word – my mom said so) to make it happen. If you do, then you will be part of a very rare and small club. This rare club has members that you would instantly recognize (Apple, Southwest Airlines, Virgin Atlantic, Disney, Amica Insurance, Ritz Carlton Hotels), and while they do have competition, they are so far ahead that competitors are always eating their service dust.

Signature service is not just about smiles and treating people well. Those are important too, but it requires an organization that is aligned and designed to be efficient and effective. One where doing the right things is not an option, it is a requirement; one that is led by sharp, caring, focused leaders who don't shirk when the going gets tough.

The Role of the Chief Executive

So, what do leaders need to do? Well, **first** they need to decide what they want and what business they are in. There must be absolutely no confusion in the minds of company leaders as to what is the number one focus of the company. Southwest Airlines is headed by Gary C. Kelly (who succeeded Herb Kelleher) and is a shining example of great service in the airline industry.

In an effort to make the government more customer-friendly, the White House consulted with Kelly along with a few other business leaders. On the topic of customer service, the conversation focused on Kelly.[85] Southwest's mission is *"dedication to the highest quality of Customer Service delivered with a sense of warmth, friendliness, individual pride and Company Spirit."* Colleen Barrette, President Emeritus of the airline, said *"We are not an airline with great customer service. We are a great customer service organization that happens to be in the airline business."* Southwest gets it; they are customer-focused and aligned. Do they have all kinds of logistic and operational challenges? I doubt there are many sectors with more of these than the commercial aviation business. But even in the airline business, they understand that EVERYTHING must be aligned to service. Without it, they might as well be an inefficient public bus on wings. It would be easy to point out a few of Southwest's so-called competitors who fit the public bus description, but I will leave this to you. The point here is that the leader must be clear on what business the company is in and what they want (highest focus).

Sam Walton was a leader who was super clear about what business Wal-Mart is in and what's the main focus. Their focus is obviously not great service quality (I have seen sporadic efforts to provide good service at Wal-Mart – but I would not describe their service as great in the least), but then that's generally true for big box retailers.

Mr. Sam (as he was called) always intended to give customers a great deal; price has always been the big draw. With this intention in mind, they set up a do-it-yourself type shopping experience, less staff on the floor, thus keeping operating costs down. I make no excuses for the service quality of most big-box retailers, but the next time you

---

[85] (Michaels 2010)

Richard Solomon

spend too much time trying to find an associate to assist you at one of these stores, remember that the system is designed for self-help. This strategy helps keep costs down, but service pays a price - the level of service quality will always be impacted because of this.

Here we see the focus of the CEO as having a major impact on the business as a whole in the long term. And while I DO NOT ADVOCATE this model, it does show that the CEO can set in train a series of events that makes things happen in a particular way.

Wal-Mart and other big-box retailers need to do a better job of leveraging ICT in their stores to help customers help themselves. Why not have a multi-language item locator that is easily accessible to shoppers? Customers can simply type in what they are looking for, the system will locate the best available options, from which the customer would choose one, and the location (aisle, row, lane, shelf, etc.) would be displayed. Or better yet, customers can have an app with a map of the store that gets the information they just selected, which in turn shows the path to get to the item. I expect that the cost of the system would be more than offset by the profit from increased sales.

Once the CEO Knows

Once the CEO is clear on what business the company is in and what they want, all other leaders need to buy into the new direction and set an example for the rest of the organization to follow. He or she needs to promote this direction/vision and gain buy-in from the top team.

The way people are led, the level of empowerment, and the personal performance of the leadership will impact any effort to create a **signature** service culture in a significant manner. So vital is this

Richard Solomon

component that, if all the other pieces of the puzzle are in place, the whole effort could flop without the right leadership. The way resources are deployed, how performance is managed, and what gets priority all fall under the purview of leadership and are things that must be tended to in order to ensure the ship is headed in the right direction. It is the leaders who design the organization to deliver the WOW, from hiring to training to measurement, rewards, product choices, and market segmentation; they are all dependent on leadership.

This effort will not succeed based on the CEO or the executive team alone. Leaders at all levels must support the cause and those who don't fit should be trained, coached, and given time to adjust; all those who do not tangibly measure up should be moved out!!! If all leaders are in the boat on the voyage, everyone needs to do their part to champion the effort. "If you are going, you better be rowing!"

If you are one who believes that the company needs this or that leader, manager, or executive for their technical competence notwithstanding their lack of focus on leadership and service, I suggest you seriously reconsider your position. Not only does this position speak to a gaping hole in your company's succession planning efforts, but what would happen if that star resigned suddenly, went to a competitor or, God forbid, got hit by a bus? Technical competence and talent may be a challenge to find, but if **signature** service is the ultimate goal, then there is to be no compromise. Leaders simply MUST HAVE **signature** service to all customers as their #1 goal. If their goal is different, then they are not aligned to the organization and if the needed change is not forthcoming, then bluntly put, these

Richard Solomon

leaders don't belong here. If this sounds harsh, that's not the intent but, **signature** service is not a matter to be toyed with and if a leader won't buy in, then we cannot afford to sacrifice the organization on the altar of one person.

The Chief Customer Officer

The position started showing up in corporate board rooms in the 1980s, and of all the C-Suite positions, the Chief Customer Officer (CCO) is most likely the newest. The logic here is simple: if the customer is an all-important asset to the company, it then follows that there should be a champion sitting at the most powerful level of the organization to design, orchestrate, and improve the customer experience.

According to the Chief Customer Officer Council, a quarter of the *Fortune* 100 have a CCO, AND a *Forbes* article in 2016 indicated that 39 percent of companies have a senior-level executive "leading the charge on customer experience." Much is yet to be done to clarify the role of the CCO, and while there are strong arguments for and against the role itself, everyone agrees that someone at the table of chiefs must be accountable for the customer. Just as the Chief People Officer is responsible for all things "people," so too is the CCO responsible for all things "customer." The CCO position has overall responsibility for the customer experience through all channels of delivery.

The CCO role does not usually oversee a fully functional group like other operational departments. However, there are instances where the CCO has a significant operational department sitting under them. One such example would be a telecom where the call center reports into this position. In many other cases, the role dovetails into others to ensure that the overall organization strategy is developed and executed with the customer in mind. Specifically, the CCO role is usually responsible for:

1. Bringing customers to life by ensuring their interests are carefully considered in strategy and decision making and execution; this includes customer insight management.

2. Injecting a new way of thinking about and acting toward the customer across the organization.

3. Improving and unifying all customer initiatives and processes across different functions.

4. Developing a common understanding of what being customer-centric means.

5. Uniting the C-suite as leaders in any customer-related transformation.

6. Imbedding competencies to initiate and improve the customer experience.

7. Developing a culture that enables customer-centricity.

8. Enabling employees to deliver customer-focused value.

9. Mapping and measuring customer experience.

Here are some examples of how the role comes to life: The CCO must ensure that all customer-facing processes are designed to bring maximum ease to the customer, this will also dovetail with the role of the Chief Operating Officer. Ensuring that products are designed to meet customer needs and preferences will require collaborative efforts with R&D, Product Development and Engineering. Yet another might be to ensure that the quality of interactions is in keeping with the

Richard Solomon

organization's vision and experience map. This will possibly require work with HR, Training, and Operations. One more could be ensuring that the customer experience online is engaging and seamless, which requires the efforts of IT.

The person filling the CCO position needs certain competencies to be effective:

1. **Visionary** – Can *develop and hold a huge customer-focused vision of the organization.*

2. **Futurist** – *Can envisage the future and predict customer needs and preferences.*

3. **Strategist** – *Able to develop and orchestrate the execution of critical organization moves to achieve the vision.*

4. **Leader** – *Able to influence people through trust-building, role-modeling and communication.*

5. **Politician** – *Be persuasive with a wide variety of stakeholders with different needs and objectives.*

6. **Advisor** – *Provide wise counsel to senior managers and other members of the C-Suite on customer issues.*

7. **Advocate** – *Thinking like a customer and representing this along with analytical information in the right places and to the right people.*

8. **Analyst** – *Make meaning of customer data and information to inform business strategies and moves.*[86]

---

[86] (Trevail 2016)

Richard Solomon

But is the Leadership Serious?

The CEO of a large supermarket chain once asked to meet with me, after he heard of some of the work my firm had done with another retail company. He was seeking my help in "developing a service culture." I was elated at the request and hoped that we would be able to help him steer his ship into beautiful waters of **signature** service.

The meeting was interesting, as he told me they wanted to create "a customer service culture" and exactly how to do it (my mind asked, if you know how to do it, why call me?). Essentially, he wanted my firm to provide <u>training</u> to all his front store staff, full stop. While we could have easily done that, I informed him that doing so would not get him the culture he sought for the company. I then proceeded to explain some of the components involved. I sent him a one-page discussion paper summarizing the approach to be taken. I never heard from him or any of his people after this; there was just too much work involved. Needless to say, their service quality remains the same today – not bad, just bland. Too many leaders aren't ready to suit up and show up, because changing the service culture of a firm or a major business unit takes backbone, it takes strength, it takes time, it requires belief and focus, and it requires hope! If it were easy to do, then everyone would do it.

Rightly, the world puts amazing pressures on leaders to produce; stock markets can be very fickle, and panic is often an investment strategy. A couple of bad decisions or a few poor quarters could signal the beginning of the end for the CEO or the firm as a whole. In his book *The 21 Irrefutable Laws of Leadership*, John Maxwell talks

Richard Solomon

about The Law of the Lid.[87] If the leader cannot see a vision of a customer-centered organization that provides consistent **signature** service, then it's going to be hard (near impossible) for the rest of the organization to suit up and take aim at this lofty goal. Leaders go first!

Making Your Own Business Case

A few years ago, I helped a large multi-national telecom make their own business case for this. As we walked through the analysis, the numbers and hemorrhage shocked the executives, for they simply did not realize the extent of the impact that poor service was having. They decided to invest millions of dollars to close the wound, and my company helped them to clarify the strategy, coach the leaders, and train the staff. They have seen an amazing return on investment in the years that followed.

You should always start with the business case. Back in chapter 2, I outlined several strong arguments for delivering **signature** service; let's bring some of these to life. Executing **The Signature Service Strategy and developing a Service Culture** will take time, money and effort. The simplest and most direct way to look at this is that poor service creates various opportunity costs and operational expenses. You are either spending more than you need to, or dealing with lost potential sales; either way you lose.

Firstly, there is the actual revenue lost when a customer leaves. If we calculate the customer lifetime value[88] lost, this can really add up. Also remember that it is much easier to sell to people who have

---

[87] (Maxwell 2007)
[88] The average value of the customer's transaction per year multiplied by the amount of years the customer could potentially remain active

Richard Solomon

already bought from you, and they tend to spend more than new customers. Better service allows companies to charge higher prices, as customers don't mind paying more for the increased value.

Secondly, is the reputation risk and damage to the service image. Remember that 90 percent of the public forms its opinion of a company based on service. People spread the news about bad service fast, far, and wide, and with the use of social media and customer complaint web pages, it's even worse. Also, a large percentage (90 percent) of customers believe that the level of service they receive is important when deciding whether to do business with a company. Naturally, reputation loops back into sales, and it has the huge potential of changing how the whole market views your brand.

Thirdly, there is all the added cost when customers leave. The actual effort to close out an account includes taking the call or visit, time for discussing the issue, finding them on the system, and going through the close-out process. In some cases and industries, the customer just never returns and there is no actual close-out process. A major cost when customers defect is finding new ones with enormous marketing budgets seeking to replace defectors. Marketing is fine, but much of the marketing budget is wasted. I remember one CEO saying: "half of the money we spend on marketing is wasted, we just don't know which half." Money spent plugging the hemorrhage of lost customers due to poor service is always a sure thing.

Richard Solomon

What to do:

As a leader, it is not always easy to gain support for initiatives in the C-Suite or at any level for that matter; you must present arguments that are cogent, solid and well thought out. Remember that organizations always have competing priorities and you must be able to justify the resource allocation and attention needed. Use the points below to make your own business case. One stand-out point is that customer focus positively impacts every part of the business; truthfully, everyone wins.

Lost Revenue or Opportunities

1. What percentage of your customers believe that your company **exceeds their service expectations?**

    a. Check customer satisfaction scores for the past three years. If you don't have these scores, you need to start gathering data now! If you need support here in terms of developing a customer feedback system, go to *www.thesignatureservicestrategy.com,* navigate to the "downloads" section and sign up for the free guide or template. Or just contact us and we can help.

2. How much more would your customers **be willing to pay** to ensure a great service experience? How many will pay for the premium? This greatly depends on your target market and the type of product. But even if you went with the lowest statistic of 44 percent paying 5 percent more, this can represent a great addition to the bottom line.

Richard Solomon

3. Calculate the **customer lifetime value** of your best, longstanding customers (Customer Lifetime Value = Average repeat customer transaction value X amount of transactions per year X expected length of lifetime in years).

Reputation Risk

1. Go digging to discover and categorize the reasons *your* customers leave. What percentage is due to poor service? Typically, this sits around 64 percent.

2. What percentage of your customer complaints are resolved in the customers' favor? 70% of complaining customers will do business with you again if you resolve in their favor.

3. What percentage of your customer complaints are resolved on-the-spot? Remember that on-the-spot resolutions increases the willingness of customers to continue doing business with your company up to 90%.

Added Costs

1. Find out what customer defection is costing your company annually. You can include:

   a. Cost of taking account-ending calls or visits.

   b. The cost of closing out accounts.

   c. The cost to replace the defectors (customers who left).

   d. The cost of accepting returns.

   e. Negative impact on cash flow and finance cost to boost liquidity.

If for one minute there is doubt in your mind or organization that there is most likely a service problem – and opportunity, **start here**.

What to Do

1. Make your own business case (see above).
2. Decide what business you are in.
3. Establish a clear service vision.
4. Get clear on your role as a leader in this service mission.
5. Understand how **signature** service can be used as a strategic weapon.
6. Enroll other leaders – If you are going, you better be rowing!
7. Be a servant leader – enable others to do their best work.
8. Align resources, processes, and systems to making the vision a reality.
9. Have a heart for the organization.

Summary

Whether you sit in the C-Suite or are another senior manager, leaders go first. If you want others to be on this journey, you must take point on the mission. Leadership is about going somewhere (a destination) and taking people (the followers) with you. Think then, how do you know where you are going if you don't have a vision? Leaders, boldly step out front and declare that the organization is first about service, they set vision, the example and facilitate the organization's **signature** service work through alignment, resource allocation and servant leadership.

Richard Solomon

Chapter 5

Listen to the Voice of Your Customers

Listening to the **Voice of your Customer** (VOC) should be a way of life. After all, isn't service really about giving customers more of what they want in the way they want it? Too many companies behave like customers are some kind of afterthought or necessary evil; you sometimes get the feeling that *"we want your money, but we don't want you."*

With only 1 in 26 dissatisfied customers willing to complain out loud, you run the risk of the other 25 just walking away without giving you the opportunity to solve the problem or make valuable changes, a whopping 96 percent! This is like leaving money on the table; remember the lifetime value of the customer is so much more than any one transaction. Sure, customers are not always clear about what they want or are sometimes not able to articulate it well. But despite these, there is no one better to ask than the customer himself.

Customer-Specificity

Products aside, what makes a customer experience excellent and thus creates **signature** service is really dependent on what your customer values the most. To coin a phrase, I call this customer-specificity: *"The individual view of a customer as to what makes the service to him or*

Richard Solomon

her excellent." For me, (aside from the product itself) the components that make service excellent are: speed, accuracy, focus, ease, pleasant interaction, and flexibility. While most customers would want these in their service formula, some may change the priority order, add another item, or remove some items completely.

Listening to the Voice of the Customer

Let us examine what it means to listen to the voice of the customer.

1. It is about knowing who they are

There is a very stark difference between a customer and an ideal customer. Many years ago (far more than I care to count), as we sat in a Principles of Business class as 4th form (Grade 9) students, the teacher helped us to understand what demand is in business. If my memory serves me right, Mr. Dos Santos asked the class what was demand. We quickly responded, "when someone wants to buy something." While desire is important, he clarified that you needed something else to make it to the demand category and that was the ability to pay. His example went something like this: how many of you would like a brand-new BMW? Almost all hands went up. How many of you could pay for one? No hands went up. In very much the same fashion, anyone who pays for your product or service can be considered a customer. However, not everyone who pays is your ideal client or fits into one of your ideal client segments.

Richard Solomon

This is where the concept of the customer avatar[89] comes into play. Very few businesses can create individual approaches to serve each and every customer. At best, what companies seek to do is serve segments or groupings of customers, or in some cases – a single ideal client.

Many banks now offer the still-illusive Black Card; gone are the days when Gold was the elite standard, I guess black is the new gold. Visa, for example, has a Black Card that they call their Signature Card for their VIP customers. The list of perks is mouth-watering: 24-hour international concierge service, travel insurance, car-rental insurance, travel miles rewards, travel medical insurance (for card holder and family), worldwide replacement of lost cards, travel insurance for luggage, and a VIP lounge program. The Black Card is by invitation only and your purchasing power has to be in the range of $250K per annum. Clearly not for everyone, is it?

In creating this product, Visa had to get crystal clear on the profile of their ideal client or customer avatar. Age, occupations, income, lifestyle, life-stage, interests, education levels, and so on. As many of the benefits are focused on travel, obviously Visa did their homework and recognized that travel was a significant part their ideal customers' lives – hence all the travel related benefits and the built-in conveniences.

---

[89] The avatar is a composite of major, unique relevant commonalities of your ideal customers

Richard Solomon

If you gather information on the customer-specificity of your ideal client group(s), you will begin to see trends and themes that will enable you to serve them better. They will tell you what they want and need.

2. It is about making it easy for them to give their opinion

Companies are generally horrible at the implementation and use of customer feedback systems. When last did you fill in a survey or one of those feedback cards and got an actual response? If you are like most people, you don't even bother to fill them in, as you hardly expect the service to improve.

My advice to clients is "go asking for trouble;" take the bitter with sweet. Don't wait for the customer to seek out an opportunity to give feedback, make it easy, make it available, make it ongoing. Sure, I know, we don't like bad news and your people are trying really hard, but these are not good reasons for not proactively seeking out the feedback from your customers.

Have multiple passive channels, like a button on the site that takes them to a place to complain or give praise, and those in-store cards that can be filled out in a minute. But you need to have active systems which purposefully ask customers what they like and what they would like. These must be easily accessible and useable so that customers are more inclined to use them than not. Your people also need to understand why this is important and offer them to customers on a regular basis. They are more inclined to do this when they understand

Richard Solomon

how the information will be used — developmentally and not punitively. A great touch is to give a reward of some kind for their participation, this is best in the form of a discount on their next purchase or a coupon for use in-store as it increases the likelihood that the customer will return.

3. It is about asking the right questions

"I am sorry, my responses are limited, you have to ask the right questions." – Dr. Alfred Lanning (I, Robot).

Like in the case of fictional character quoted here, when seeking customer feedback, you have to be careful to ask the right questions. Remember customers have many sources competing for their attention and time.

Long after the excitement and novelty of the purchase has worn off, the customer remembers how they felt during the interaction with your service providers and systems. This is not to say that the product is unimportant, you need a decent product, preferably a great one, but poor service spoils a great product.

In 2006, I purchased a second-generation VW Touareg. The VW Group is a German car conglomerate and the parent company of such big names Porsche, Bentley, Lamborghini, Bugatti and Audi. The Touareg shares much of its base architecture with the Porsche Cayenne, and many of the parts are similar and fit these and the Audi Q7.

The Touareg was originally designed as a true off-road vehicle with amazing torque. *The vehicle was named after the*

Richard Solomon

nomadic Tuareg people, inhabitants of the Saharan interior in North Africa and a tribe notorious for strength and adaptability, the traits that Volkswagen decided to infuse into their Touareg[90].

I recall seeing one pull a Boeing 747 in a YouTube video as I did my research on the SUV before purchase. The thing is built like a tank, heavy and powerful, but luxurious and handles ever so gently. The reviews were generally great, with the occasional issue here or there. Once I did a test drive, I was sold, decision made, order placed!

The car had some quality issues, as the wheel alignment refused to stay in place, the air conditioning up and quit, buttons and switches faded quickly and then there was the hood lining that came undone after a relatively short time. The thing is that none of these were as annoying as the dealer's general approach to the service. Best Auto is a subsidiary of the Neal and Massy Group (NM); the auto division of NM is a behemoth of an organization (by local terms), called Neal and Massy Motors. Its origins date back to 1969 and they account for 40 percent of the passenger car market in Trinidad and Tobago.[91]

On the website, they list "Customer Importance" as one of their values. When I was making arrangements to purchase the car, I remember cautioning the then-GM that a great car is easily spoiled by poor service. Naturally he went to town and

---

[90] (Chan 2016)
[91] (Massy Motors Automotive Limited 2018)

Richard Solomon

back to allay my concerns, "this is our flagship vehicle," he said, and "we pull out all the stops to ensure superior service," he assured.

My biggest complaint about that experience was not the car itself, although many of these issues are completely unacceptable for the VW Group. My complaint was the time it took to get matters sorted out and the availability of spares and other parts. Now to be fair, some of the issues I raised above were repaired outside of warranty, but how is it possible that you are the lone dealer for a brand and do not stock simple parts like sensors, filters, bulbs or a dipstick? Why on God's green earth would it take 6–12 weeks to get any of these parts? And while I am at it, why should it cost as much as 10 times more for a part that I could easily order online and have in hand in one week?

Best Auto certainly did not single me out for this treatment nor did NM; but despite my repeated complaints and admonitions, nothing significantly changed. Why not listen to the voice of the customer? Now I know I don't understand all the complexities of the supply chain and optimal stock levels for an auto dealer; not only don't I understand, I also don't care! As customers, what we want is for our issues to be sorted out smoothly and easily and guess what? The organization that does that best is most likely to get the repeat business. Despite all of this, I bumped my head one day and thought of ordering a new Touareg (I really like the vehicle), but when I thought of

Richard Solomon

all the challenges with the dealer – no way Jose (the salesperson's name was not Jose by the way).

If Best Auto and the wider NW Auto Group had bothered to ask, they would have realized that customers like me were tired of seeing "no stock" on estimates and would rather not have to source our own parts from the UK, Germany, Poland, Spain, USA and any other place that seemed to get it to me faster (a big shout out to Cesar Mir at Palmetto 57 VW in Opa-locka, FL). When you ask the right questions and act on the answers, it translates into profits. Not only will I not be buying another Touareg, but also I won't replace our second car (a VW Passat) with another of its kind. And despite their urgings, I will not be replacing my Ford pick-up truck with the VW Amarok.

According to research by Cint, 62 percent of consumers are more likely to buy from a brand that asks their opinion.[92] Use the passive and active systems mentioned before, give your customers a reasonable discount on their next purchase for filling in a survey, hire a college student and have them ask customers as they browse the store or while they wait in line, place a pop-up on your site inviting customers to answer a short survey before they check out or leave. There are dozens of ways to get customer feedback.

Here are some useful sample questions to repeatedly ask your customers:

---

[92] (Burns 2012)

Richard Solomon

1. Would you recommend us to a friend?

2. What's the one (or 3) big thing(s) that nearly stopped you from using us?

3. What could we do to make our service to you excellent?

4. Tell us about your favorite service experience.

5. What is the one thing that we do that you wish we would stop?

6. What is your most recent example of how we exceed your expectations?

7. How can we make this transaction/process easier for you?

8. How can we help save you time/money/stress?

9. What made you buy from us in the first place?

10. How does our service compare to your expectations?

11. How likely are you to purchase from us the next time around (why or why not)?

12. In three words, describe your interaction with our people.

This is not meant to be an exhaustive list, nor is it intended to ask all the questions your organization may need to ask. They should however prime the pump and get you going, if you need more help, let us know at *www.thesignatureservicestrategy.com*.

It is about putting their opinion first

"There is only one boss. The customer. And he can fire everybody in the company from the chairman on down, simply by spending his money somewhere else." – Sam Walton.

Richard Solomon

It matters very little who you are, what you make or sell, how long you have been in business, what last quarter's results looked like, etc. The fact is that the most important person in your business operation is the customer, for a change in their buying pattern can spell disaster.

In chapter two, I made the business case for **signature** service. The power of service and its value to the organization is impossible to be overstated. Blockbuster (the one-time video and game rental giant) learned this lesson the hard way, their demise was in part due to a failure to adopt the new technology of online streaming, which in itself was a service issue. But more importantly, Blockbuster had adopted a somewhat adversarial model toward its customers, charging them exorbitant late fees and not responding to what customers seemed to want. By the time Netflix came around, Blockbuster's efforts to compete were too little, too late; they now had such a bad reputation of not putting the customers' opinion first that the market was not willing to give them a chance. They shut down half their stores and were eventually auctioned off to Dish Network in bankruptcy court in 2011.[93]

Someone recently told me that Blockbuster's high late fees were to discourage customers from incurring them in the first place. A Blockbuster manager told them that "having a movie out of stock (due to late returns) alienated an average of five other customers who would come in to rent that movie and go away unhappy." Let's say for a moment that they were right;

---

[93] (Fritz 2011)

Richard Solomon

taking such a punitive angle with customers was no way to solve the problem. Clearly customers were expressing a need by returning movies later than agreed, plus their loud complaints about the fees *still* needed to be addressed. How was Blockbuster putting their customers first by spanking them with these exorbitant late fees? It only says to me that they had a habit of not listening to the voice of the customer.

No one can say for sure, but I would bet good money that Blockbuster would have had a fighting chance had they treated their customers better and paid attention to the trends. The customer outcry was there but they refused to listen. Remember; put the customers' opinion first.

Samsung phone owners swear by their smart devices, because the screen display is vivid, they run the Android operating software, and are thus more open for configuration to individual tastes. Contrast this with the iPhone; many users will tell you that iPhones do not play nice with others, the IOS platform is more closed, if you want to share music or pictures with a user on another platform, you generally need to go through an intermediary.

Still, Apple is very clear on the value proposition and what *their* customers want most. They want a stable platform that is fairly intuitive, which is secure and handles the basics well. Whether you are a fan or not, the fact is that Apple remains the largest company in the world by market capitalization, with

Richard Solomon

the iPhone accounting for almost 70 percent of sales, an obvious cash cow,[94] see infographic 27 below.

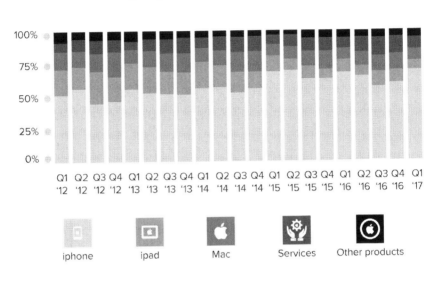

APPLE'S REVENUE BY PRODUCT
category Q1 2012 to Q1 2017

Infographic 27

There is no shortage of criticism of the iPhone, but Apple has stuck to its guns, providing products and service that *their* customers want. Sure, they could pay attention to what critics and others are saying, but Apple knows who pays the bills and who butters their bread. They are not swayed by general public opinion; they put the opinion of *their* customers above all else and simply make products that *their customers will buy.*

---

[94] (Econ243 2017)

Richard Solomon

It is about making meaning of the feedback

The only purpose of gathering customer feedback is so that you can improve your service to them. What about if all they have to say are compliments, you ask? If that is the case, then you have not asked enough customers, and/or you are not asking the right questions. This is not to say that you should not accept compliments, far from it; however, if all you get are compliments, you are doing something wrong in terms of the actual data gathering.

The nature of human behavior makes it virtually impossible for customers to be impressed or even satisfied with a specific level of service or product over the medium to long-term. This desire for more is seemingly insatiable, even when it comes to quality of service.

A few years ago, I consulted with a client in the telecom sector on a variety of customer-focused issues including churn, service quality, and aligning strategy to service vision. In those days, broadband speeds were slow when compared with today's fiber-to-the-home systems. They had just greatly increased the speed to customers, and everyone got an upgrade at no added cost. They were proud, and customers were happy.

As we discussed the implications of this and the added strain it would place on the systems as more customers came into the fold, the director of marketing and I quickly came to the realization that we needed to move the group out of celebratory mood and into planning for the next move, as soon

Richard Solomon

this would become *"the new normal."* This term became a go-to description for us over the next few years: Once something became normal, customers would soon seek out the next level of speed and service. We knew that customers would continue to demand more and hitting a new level of service was never enough to allow the organization to rest.

Customer feedback needs to be put through a sense-making or analytical exercise to convert it to usable information. What are the customers really saying? What message are they sending you? The lens through which you view the data will depend on what business you are in" Telecoms are different from retail, for example; whether your service is delivered to the customer in-person versus online; the type of customer giving the feedback — dormant, active, new, long-term; and the volume of the feedback and thereby how reliable the emerging story is.

An added point here is the motivation of customers for giving feedback. Don't be surprised if there a tendency of the data to cluster around appalling and excellent; this is particularly true when feedback is unsolicited, as people have a greater motivation to give feedback when they have extreme experiences. Look at some of the restaurant reviews on Yelp, for example, and you may see this trend.

Another way you can gain added meaning from the data is by comparing it to that of your closest rivals. Be wary of this, however, and be sure that you are comparing like with like. Survey questions differ, and customer segments vary. A more

Richard Solomon

important point of examination is to compare the data with your customer excellence vision; what is the gap here? Spend time with the data – even have a third party look at it to find the themes and trends.

It is about acting on their voice

Have you seen the great efforts some organizations make to boast about their customer service statistics? In some cases, I have thought that the numbers didn't reflect the experiences I had with them! Who is giving these rankings? Are they fudging the numbers? Was I singled out for some poor service experiment? Maybe those other customers went to the branch all the way across town.

Let's assume your company scored 9 (1 – 10 scale) in a particular area of measurement, meaning that the average customer must have been very satisfied with whatever is being measured, right? Well on the surface, you would be right. After all, 90 percent is a great score on any test and something to celebrate. Celebrate if you want, but be sure to spend time too on what you could have done differently to score the extra 10 percent. What you should now ask and figure out is what must happen so that the 90 percent can turn into 110 percent. The service giants are never satisfied with almost perfect scores.

If you accept that **signature** service is the most important business strategy and that it is really the customers who make or break the business, then it follows that their voice should influence how the business is run. My suggestion is to use

Richard Solomon

customer feedback to influence and improve every aspect of the organization: Product design, who gets hired, training, pricing, marketing strategy, sales channels, rewards and recognition, and on and on and on. This effort is not an annual event, nor is it something you do because your last quarter results were below prediction. This is an ongoing, never-ending effort; just like you want to sell every day, you should also want to hear from your customers continuously. Be obsessive about it, don't be casual, behave like feedback from customers is a life-and-death matter. In fact, it is.

Sons of Maxwell

Dave Carroll belongs to a music band called Sons of Maxwell. In 2008, on a United Airlines flight from Halifax, Canada to Omaha, Nebraska via Chicago's O'Hare airport, he had the experience of a lifetime. The passenger behind him exclaimed: "My God they're throwing guitars out there!" To Dave's and his band mates' horror, they saw their guitar cases being abusively tossed around by the baggage handlers (if you have never seen baggage handlers load and unload luggage, I advise that you avoid seeing it).

Complaints to the cabin crew got him passed to an Acting Lead Agent who in turn passed him to someone else. Long story short, by the time they got to Halifax, Carroll found that his $3,500 Taylor 710 guitar had been badly damaged. This is where the story gets interesting; despite his insistence and efforts, United Airlines refused to pay for the damaged guitar. Dave went on to write and perform the hit

Richard Solomon

song "United Breaks Guitars," which had over 3.5M views in ten[95] days with the current viewer total on YouTube pushing close to 20M.[96]

BBC News reported that, as a result of the PR disaster, United Airlines' share price fell by 10 percent, reducing the company value by some $180M! United has since tried to compensate for the damage and has said they would like to use the song and video for training purposes to ensure that all customers have a better service experience from the company in the future.[97] It's interesting to note that United Airlines is ranked lowest among the big airlines in the American Customer Satisfaction Index.[98]

Dave Carroll has gone on to launch a whole new career as a speaker and author. But United could have prevented all this mess by simply listening to the voice of the customer in the first place. Actually, they should have treated the customer's property with some more respect. They boast that 99.something percent of luggage arrives undamaged, but they failed to take into account the point-something percent that does get damaged.

---

[95] (Carroll 2012)
[96] (Sons of Maxwell 2009)
[97] (BBC News 2009)
[98] (Picchi 2017)

Richard Solomon

"When customers share their story, they're not just sharing pain points. They're actually teaching you how to make your product, service, and business better. Your customer service organization should be designed to efficiently communicate those issues." - Kristin Smaby, *Being Human is Good Business.*[99]

United Breaks More than Guitars

It would seem that United has not learned the lesson. In early 2017, they denied boarding to two children as they deemed their leggings to be inappropriate (leggings???? seriously!!!). But the worst was yet to come. On April 9, 2017, flight 3411 from Chicago to Louisville was overbooked, which is not an uncommon situation. It is reported that there were staff members who "needed" to fly and three passengers were "randomly selected" for removal after no one took up the offers for travel vouchers (a maximum of $1000.00) to voluntarily deplane and take the next flight the following day.

Security officers were called in to forcibly eject Dr. David Dao – a resident of Louisville Kentucky, from the flight. He steadfastly resisted, explaining that he had patients to see the next morning. He can be seen in the viral video first making his case to someone (presumably a United CSR) before being dragged, bloodied and semi-conscious, off the flight as other passengers expressed their disgust and horror at the officers'

---

[99] (Lloyd 2016)

Richard Solomon

actions.[100] In the days that followed, United's CEO described the screaming Dr. Dao as "disruptive" and "belligerent."

Not only did United create a firestorm of negative publicity, they chose to refund every passenger, and settled with Dr. Dao for an undisclosed sum, which is estimated to be in the millions.[101] Their stock price lost 4.3 percent in the days that followed, almost 1 billion dollars in value!!! [102]

What to Do

1. Get clear on whom your customers really are.
2. Carefully craft your questions.
3. Make it easy for customers to give you feedback
4. Put their opinions first.
5. Make meaning out of that feedback
6. Take action based on the feedback.

Summary

The voice of the customer has always been powerful, but social media, video sharing and the ease of setting up a webpage or site has made it super-easy for every Tim, Duke, and Henry to communicate to millions of other customers about their experiences.

This VOC concept must be a formally imbedded component of the organization's way of doing business and culture. If we are measuring the right things, we must use that information to make the organization better, information must not just sit around collecting

---

[100] (ABC News 2017)
[101] (Mindock 2017)
[102] (Udland 2017)

dust, all measurements must have a purpose, for they are never ends unto themselves. Listen to the voice of the customer, remember, they are the reason you "open the doors" every day.

If you need more help here in terms of developing a customer feedback system, go to *www.thesignatureservicestrategy.com*. See chapter 9 for more on mapping, measuring and managing the customer experience.

Richard Solomon

Chapter 6

Hire Right

"Never try to teach a pig to sing; it wastes your time and it annoys the pig."

Paul Dickson

Service giants understand that <u>you can't make diamonds out of mud,</u> and while training is important and necessary, if you have the wrong people in the first place, it's improbable for you to get the kind of outcome (**signature** service) that your company wants, and your customers deserve.

Some time ago, I went to Orlando, Florida to deliver the keynote to a group of senior managers and executives of a telecom that serves customers in several states in the US. The CEO had heard me speak at a large conference in Puerto Rico and invited me to be the featured speaker at their annual management retreat. I live in Trinidad and Tobago, which is located (at the nearest point) just 8 miles from the South American mainland, so my route to Orlando was Piarco International Airport to Miami International Airport then to Orlando International Airport (POS-MIA; MIA-MCO for you frequent fliers).

I flew business class on American Airlines, as flying up front is generally a nicer experience and certainly more spacious than the

Richard Solomon

economy seats further back. The service is noticeably better, although certainly not **signature**.

I landed in Orlando right on time, got my bags, and went to the rental garage where a mid-sized SUV was waiting with my name on it. I generally prefer to drive when I have speaking engagements like this one, as it gives me a nice degree of flexibility of movement (not to mention I can find a coffee shop early in the morning and enjoy a hot cup away from the hotel crowd).

I know Orlando because we have spent some of our summer vacations there. I guess it's like TV, you often end up on the kids' channels not because the programming interests you very much, it's just what my children watch so the programming is familiar. Orlando is sort of like that — very familiar to me.

Anyway, I grabbed the rental, popped on the GPS and was off. All of these events were pretty much normal, and it was when I arrived at the hotel where the retreat was being held that I got a shot of **signature** service!

The Waldorf Astoria Orlando is a beautiful hotel; at the time it was the newest of the Waldorf Hotels and sits on 482 pristine acres in Bonnet Creek. The area is mostly filled with hotels, resorts, and theme parks; lawns and hedges are constantly manicured, and colors are brighter than the bland you see in other places, bright enough to stand out without disturbing all the natural shades of flora found just everywhere.

I think I got in around 4:30 p.m. and drove directly to the hotel. As I maneuvered the mid-size SUV up to the huge front entrance, I could see several well-dressed stewards and bellhops waiting to welcome

　　　　　Richard Solomon

guests. I noticed how they speedily moved (almost running) to meet *their* new guests; this is where I coined the phrase "tripping-over-themselves-service." I was greeted with what I presume to be the standard welcome (although it felt genuine and specific to me), you could see that there was a real person behind the smiling eyes, not this plastic "welcome to wherever" or "enjoy your meal" that you get in so many other places.

I was offered valet parking, but because I am generally skeptical about service upsells (I often find them disappointing), I asked the valet exactly what was I getting. The service pro was happy to efficiently answer my questions, so warm, welcoming, and effective was his manner that I would have taken the upsell even if I did not really want it. He was quick, deft, and smoothly slipped in that no matter how many times I needed the car brought around, they would be happy to do it. All I needed to do was phone a little ahead.

I got out of the car and made my way through the luxurious lobby. As the clock that sat atop the large dial in the middle of the floor came into view, I could see my bags on their way to the front desk where the check-in was equally pleasant and smooth.

Everyone I dealt with for the full extent of my stay seemed attentive, willing, and knowledgeable. Another thing that I noted was that everyone called me by name; several times I checked to see if I was wearing a name tag, but no, somehow they were able to keep track.

It has to be safe to presume that the Waldorf Astoria Orlando must have a pretty stringent and robust recruitment (and training) process

Richard Solomon

to get so many people to work in such harmony and display such welcoming warmth.

My keynote went amazingly well, the topic was "Winning the customer war through service excellence," and I could not help but include the quality service at the resort as an example to my audience. There was so much agreement in the room that a spontaneous round of applause went up for the great quality of service we were receiving!

About 100 people filled the room and as usual several stayed back to talk with me when I was done. One manager asked, "where is your book?" He went on to say that my lessons are so powerfully simple, and that it would be great to have them all in one place. Now you have them all in one place.

Don't Hire Customer-Haters

Maybe haters is too strong a word, but if you are not careful, your organization could get filled up with people who don't display much care for your customers and, trust me, you do not want that! The examples below are just snippets of experiences customers have had to endure because of the uncaring attitude of staff:

1. The waitress at a Hilton Hotel who scolded a guest because he took two packets of brown sugar from another table that had already been set for breakfast.

2. The airline supervisor who rudely refused to waive a small fee so a passenger could get on an earlier flight, even though the plane was half-empty, there was no fare difference and the passenger had no checked luggage.

Richard Solomon

3. The airline CSR who nonchalantly insisted that a family of four adults must share a standard hotel room after waiting two hours to be processed due to a flight cancellation.

4. The tax office clerk who shouted at an entire line of waiting taxpayers because they were waiting to be called to the window after each person was served, instead of going forward without being called.

5. The airline agent who ignored a customer waiting to make a payment for a full 5 minutes, constantly looking down at her computer screen.

Each of the examples above is about one thing and one thing only, and that is the attitude of the people who provided the service.

There is no such thing as a perfect hire/employee; if there were, then they would have to be perfect people to begin with. But when hiring for **signature** service, the most valuable approach in my experience is to hire for attitude. Now I am in no way suggesting that skills, qualifications, experience and other such attributes do not matter. They sure do. But if an employee has all these in profusion and the right attitude is in short supply, in my experience, you have started on a losing service journey.

The Importance of Attitude

In human behavioral terms, attitude is the tendency to respond positively or negatively to persons, ideas, challenges, and situations. In large measure, a person's attitude is self-determined; the adult therefore "decides" how he or she will respond.

Organizations spend millions of dollars to attract new customers. One of the statistics we saw before is that it costs five times as much to attract a new customer versus keeping an existing one. Now take careful note; all the effort and marketing spend can be undone and wasted in an instant – just by the attitude of your customer-facing staff. In my experience, very few organizations are careful enough in the hiring of their front-liners.

Maybe another way to think about this situation is as follows: let's imagine for a minute you were the CEO of an electricity company. As part of your company's green diversification project, a decision was made to install several 2-megawatt wind turbines over the next five years, each costing about 2M USD. Staffing for this new venture is key, since you just can't hire any person with a degree in engineering to be in charge of this plant. Nor can you hire just any technician to support the maintenance effort, can you?

The above scenario sounds ludicrous; after all, such a huge investment and important asset should not be toyed with!!! Well that is just as ludicrous as hiring someone with limited people skills and a poor attitude to take care of your most important asset – the customer. All of the investment you make to get them in the door, in your state-of-the art systems, in the marketing of leading products you sell, could be rendered unimportant in an instant. One Chief Customer Officer puts it this way: "Hire for will, train for skill."

Service All Night Long

As the South African Airways (SAA) A340 Airbus climbed out of the O.R Tambo Airport in Johannesburg, passengers gazed out as the ground drifted farther and farther away. Some stole a chance to grab a

Richard Solomon

quick pic of the airport from above. They knew that cell phones, along with all other electronic devices, should be turned off and stowed away for takeoffs and landings. As the jumbo jet climbed closer to our target cruising altitude of 40,000 feet, I had a very interesting experience. The purser began to give some information designed to make our 15-hour flight to JFK in New York "more comfortable."

"There will be two meals served on this flight, one a soon as we reach our cruising altitude and the other about 2 hours before we land in New York," he said with practiced ease. But what caught my attention was when he specifically indicated said "the crew on this flight will be on duty for the entire journey. Should you require anything in addition to our meal and beverage service, please call us and we will be too happy to accommodate your request."

Now, 15 hours is a long time to be trapped in a metal tube at 40,000 feet, flying at a speed of 570 mph (or 917 kph). My fellow passenger on the other side of the aisle made a remark about all the free liquor he could drink, and I halfway smiled. Not being much of a drinker, except for the odd occasion, this was not a selling point for me; but being a writer on topics like service, the all-night service was!

I generally try not to fly continuously for so many hours; trips to Africa tend to be routed through Europe, making each segment shorter and easier to bear. But here I was on a 15-hour journey heading back from Maputo Mozambique via Johannesburg with a crew that professed to be truly interested in service, even under

Richard Solomon

uncomfortable conditions (have you ever tried pushing one of those drink or meal carts up and down the aisles of an A340 Airbus?).

Michael Has a Great Attitude

Take Michael for instance. A native of Johannesburg, he did not plan on a career in aviation, but with opportunities limited and not being happy with his last job, he grasped the South African Airways opportunity with both hands. That was 21 years ago, and he is now a senior cabin attendant who exemplifies customer service. He was shocked when I approached him for a few personal comments about how he is able to be such a service hero. Michael said he was discontented with the service he received in so many other places and wished for better. He reasoned that, if he wanted better from others, he should be giving better himself. In addition, he makes the critical connection between the quality of customer service and organizational success. He said, "at this point in the company's history, we cannot afford to be lax on service; it is the difference between success and failure for **my** company." One point of note: Michael says that they are in some kind of customer-related training almost every month!

The management of SAA must be happy to have Michael aboard, for he not only talked a good talk, but displayed stellar service during every interaction, putting customers at ease with a quick wit and an easy manner that would be right at home in a 6-star hotel. Michael walks a great service walk, and delivers excellent service consistently.

Hiring Great Attitudes

I recently conducted a half-day seminar on The **Signature** Service Strategy at a conference in Montego Bay, Jamaica. There were about one hundred and fifty business leaders present from many countries. When I came to the segment on hiring right, one participant earnestly asked me: "Richard, people are very good at presenting their best self during an interview. How can I possibly know *what attitude I am hiring* from an interview?"

This is an excellent question, and unfortunately people like Michael from SAA are not a dime a dozen. The answer to the question simply is: *You can't.* It is almost impossible to identify the kind of attitude that provides the best service experiences through a simple interview alone. But before I give some recommendations about how to hire the best attitudes, let's take a minute to examine a list some of qualities of the best service pros in infographic 28 below.

Infographic 28

Richard Solomon

We know there are no perfect hires and it is hard to find anyone with all these qualities in abundance. But if you are to stand a chance of finding someone remotely close, you must know the run-of-the-mill interview simply will not uncover these crucial qualities. In fact, the interview is at best a 43 percent predictor of workplace performance, and this is where the job and person descriptions are properly done and interviewers are highly skilled. It also requires a decent candidate pool to begin with, the quality of the pool being impacted by many factors including advertising methods, the public profile of the company, the industry itself, unemployment rates and the general economy.

Typically, conditions are not ideal, which in turn may negatively impact how accurately the interview is able to identify the best candidate, and thereby on-the-job fit and productivity. Here are **ten suggestions** to help you find the best customer service pros:

1. **Accept that a bad hire is usually more costly than an empty seat**. The damage to the company's reputation and internal problems caused by a bad hire far outweigh the cost associated with leaving the position empty. For example, hiring a bad CSR can result in poor service on the front line and friction within the team.

2. **Be extra careful in developing the person description.** "If you don't know where you are going, any road will take you there." This quote from Alice in Wonderland really sums it up well, because if you are not extremely clear about what skills, experiences, qualifications, and attitude you want, you could end up with a disaster.

Richard Solomon

3. **Cast a wide net – hire 1 in 10 or even 1 in 20 suitable candidates**. This takes work, but it is worth the effort to find just the right person. Use sources that will bring you higher-quality applicants, and don't ignore current employees' recommendations as a potential source.

4. **Find candidates with values similar to the company**. There is scripture taken from The Bible in the book of Amos that says, "How can two walk together unless they be agreed?" Values are crucial as they guide so much of a person's behavior and decision making. Take for example the values of helping others and honesty; if your new hire does not share these values, trouble is on the horizon.

5. **Ask questions that get to personal values indirectly**. If you asked someone if they valued confidentiality, honesty or loyalty in an interview, naturally the answer would be yes. This is a very ineffective way to find out the truth, even asking them to describe a time they were highly confidential or loyal in a difficult situation is not a sufficient approach (albeit a better one). Instead, try using a Catch 22 scenario like this one: *Your best friend is the one who recommended you for the position of HR Assistant, you really like your job and after 6 months have settled in rather well. Your boss, the HR Manager sends you a list of names and asks for certain information from each staff member's personal record. The persons on the list are marked for retrenchment due to the planned closure of a division. Your best friend's name is on the list. Do you tell your best friend? Their response to such dilemmas will tell you more about their personal values than asking directly.*

Richard Solomon

6. **Use a psychometric or behavioral style assessment.** I like to call this "getting behind the eyes." These tools help you to understand the behavioral preferences of the candidate, they don't tell you what a person can or cannot do, but will reveal what is likely easier and more difficult for the individual. I highly recommend the Extended DISC system, as it is a valid, easily administered, flexible and reliable tool. You can also configure specific reports that will reveal greater details about behaviors related to the discipline you are hiring for (sales, service, management, training, coaching etc.). Tools such as these are not meant to be used as the sole deciding factor for hiring, this is actually unethical. Instead, they should be used as one of a few contributors to a full composite of the candidate.

7. **Conduct a behavior-based interview.** The premise here is that past behavior is one of the best predictors of future behavior. Essentially you ask the candidate to give examples of what they did in certain circumstances or situations. *"Tell me about a time when you did not agree with a company's policy regarding a customer's request and what you did?"* This could reveal how they deal with authority, if they are more the empowered type or less so, whether they just follow orders or think about what they are doing. Notwithstanding my earlier comment, about this method not being sufficient, when used in conjunction with other methods, it paints a much clearer picture.

8. **Have candidates interact in a group and discuss a touchy or controversial topic**. Monitor reactions and how

they manage themselves and group interactions. This can be very revealing and helpful if you are concerned about hiring someone who has to work well in teams. Also how they get their points across, how well they listen, and how disagreements are handled. It may also give some indication about some of their values.

9. **Include ethical dilemmas in interviews.** These are usually about making a choice between two imperfect options, one may be the easy way out, but wrong; the other may be the best, but more difficult choice. The scenario in point 5 above was one such situation, another might be: *"You witness a man rob a bank, but instead of keeping the money for himself, he donates it to a local orphanage. You know this orphanage has been struggling for funding, and the money will allow the children to receive proper food, clothing, and medical care. If you report the crime, the money will be taken away from the orphanage and given back to the bank. What would you do?"*
You could also ask them to tell you about an ethical dilemma they faced and how they dealt with it.

When using an ethical dilemma or any of these suggestions for that matter, be mindful of laws or policies that may prohibit their use, and be sensitive to certain subjects (gender, race, religion, politics etc.), there is no need to unnecessarily offend or emotionally hijack a candidate.

10. **Work sample or real play.** One of the best ways to find out how someone will deal with a situation is have them actually do it. This is particularly true when the work is of a practical nature, like dealing with a disgruntled customer on the phone

or completing a particular task. You could set up a simulation and or work situation and have them actually carry out the activity or task you are trying to assess for.

Who's Winning at Finding the Best Attitudes?

Southwest Airlines

Southwest Airlines continues to outperform its peers in so many areas. Not only are they a great model of what service should be, but they also do it profitably!!! If you know anything about the financials of airlines you know this: if you are a billionaire and want to become a millionaire, then launch an airline![103] Southwest has both an amazing financial and service history.

Southwest began operations in 1971 flying out of Love Field in Dallas, Texas (incidentally "Luv" is their Ticker symbol on the NYSE) and has been profitable for 43 straight years.

Here is the tale of the tape as at 2016 (infographic 29 – 32):

___

[103] (Murphy Jr. 2015)

Richard Solomon

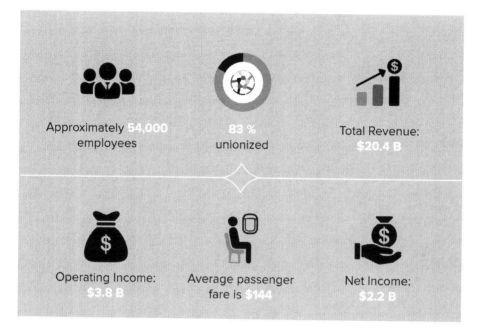

- Approximately 54,000 employees[104]
- 83 percent unionized[105]
- Total Revenue: $20.4 B
- Operating Income: $3.8 B
- Average passenger fare is $144
- Net Income: $2.2 B[106]

---

[104] (Southwest Airlines 2017b)
[105] (Southwest Airlines 2018a)
[106] (Southwest Airlines 2017b)

Richard Solomon

Largest carrier of
domestic passengers
in the USA

11ᵗʰ on Fortune's world's
most admired companies
list (top airline) 2016

Airline of the year by
Air Transport World

Air Cargo Excellence
diamond award

- Largest carrier of domestic passengers in the USA[107]
- 11 on *Fortune's* world's most admired companies list (top airline) 2016[108]
- Airline of the year by Air Transport World
- Air Cargo Excellence diamond award

---

[107] (Gulliver 2015; Bureau of Transportation Statistics 2017)
[108] (Fortune 2017)

Richard Solomon

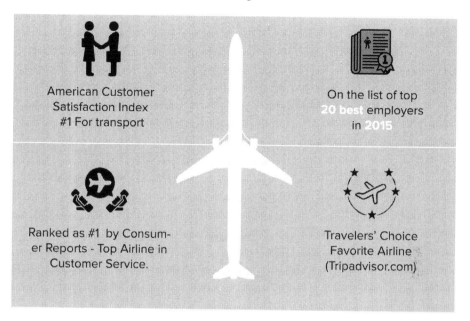

- American Customer Satisfaction Index #1 (For transport)
- On the list of top 20 best employers in 2015
- *Ranked as #1 by Consumer Reports* - Top Airline in Customer Service.
- *Travelers' Choice Favorite Airline (Tripadvisor.com)*

Richard Solomon

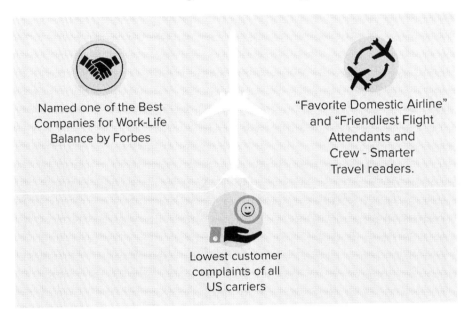

Named one of the Best Companies for Work-Life Balance by Forbes

"Favorite Domestic Airline" and "Friendliest Flight Attendants and Crew - Smarter Travel readers.

Lowest customer complaints of all US carriers

- Named one of the Best Companies for Work-Life Balance by *Forbes*
- "Favorite Domestic Airline" and "Friendliest Flight Attendants and Crew - *Smarter Travel* readers.[109]
- Lowest customer complaints of all US carriers[110]

So How Does Southwest Do It?

The Mission of Southwest Airlines is *"dedication to the highest quality of Customer Service delivered with a sense of warmth, friendliness, individual pride and Company Spirit."[111]* Notice how they put quality customer service front-and-center!!!

Remember that Southwest is a great customer service organization that happens to be in the airline business. After the September 11th

---

[109] (Southwest Airlines 2017a)
[110] (Craggs 2017)
[111] (Southwest Airlines 2018b)

Richard Solomon

attacks, many airline customers began requesting refunds because they were simply afraid of flying. Most airlines refunded the customers, less any penalties that would normally apply, but not Southwest. They issued full refund checks to passengers. Southwest made the bet that the relationship they had built up with their customers would be their saving grace and was it ever; many passengers never requested a refund, others returned their tickets saying that they did not want to fly but they did not want a refund either, while some passengers actually returned their refund checks with little notes that pretty much said: *"Keep this money, you need it more than we do and we want you to be in business in five years!!!"*[112]

How does a company (and not just any company but an airline at that) create the kind of success that Southwest has been able to create? How are they able to have not just customers but fans and brand ambassadors? Well, like all service giants, in addition to putting service upfront in everything they do (including being the first company to have a VP of Customer Service), Southwest does a number of other service fundamentals right; *one of them is to hire the right people.*

There is a quote by Robert Heinlein that goes: *"Never try to teach a pig to sing; it wastes your time and it annoys the pig."* Certainly, employees are not pigs (no nasty emails please) and humans have the distinct ability to learn and grow. But when you hire the right people, teaching them to provide **signature** service is so much easier. Southwest understands this very well. At the heart of their stellar

---

[112] (Parature Inc. 2010)

Richard Solomon

success and exemplary service are 10 organizational practices, one of these (that really supports hiring right) is: *"Hire for Attitude and Train for Skill."*

Southwest understands that 90 percent of service delivery rests in the hands of the front line; if your front-line people don't have positive attitudes and cannot manage their emotions (High EQ/EI) then you are hiring the wrong people – plain and simple.

Lisa Anderson, director of customer advocacy and communications at Southwest Airlines, says it best: "Hire for the heart and teach the task." Southwest makes very deliberate efforts to hire the right people. Here are a few of their moves to ensure that they find the right people:

1. Make no attempt to hire the most qualified or elite candidates.

2. Preference is given to candidates who will be able to integrate smoothly with other staff and teams.

3. Make a deliberate attempt to find people with the right attitudes first.

4. This approach (hiring priorities) extends to mechanics and pilots alike (unlike most other airlines).

Richard Solomon

"Something we look at is people who are very team oriented from prior work experiences. We get a feel for people who will go above and beyond. We spend more money to recruit and train than any of the other airlines do. We take the time to find the right people to hire, at all levels within our organization, and we spend time training them. We really believe in the notion of 'one bad apple.' It's like a religion here. As a result, our turnover is far less than it is at other airlines."

- Libby Saratin, former vice president of people, Southwest Airlines[113]

For years, I have preached it; most jobs are neither rocket science, nor brain surgery *(well except for rocket science and brain surgery)*, and can therefore be taught with little more than reasonable effort. But when you hire someone with a bad attitude, it's very difficult to get him or her to change. It takes personal desire for an adult human to truly change, and if someone has a negative attitude to begin with, this desire is hardly ever present. Why not stack the cards in your company's and customers' favor? Start with some high-quality people to begin with, ones who already have a positive outlook and attitude. It won't be so hard to train for most of the skills – whatever they are.

Zappos.com

This online retailer is widely reputed as being a customer-service giant, and they have done some amazing things by way of service.

---

[113] (Gittell 2005)

135 Richard Solomon

Zappos also is a generally great place to work, having been ranked #6 on *Fortune's* Best Companies to Work For in 2011.

See Zappos' tale of the tape in infographic 33 below:

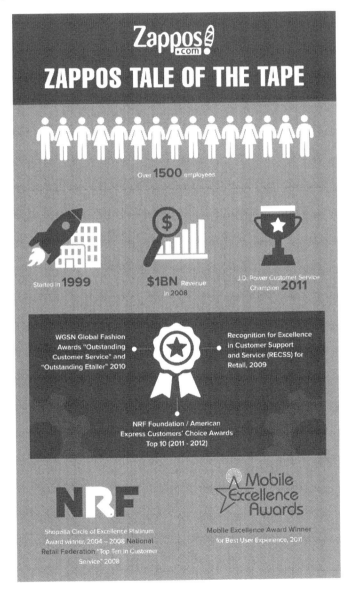

Infographic 33

Richard Solomon

- Over 1,500 employees
- Started in 1999
- Reached $1 BN in revenue in 2008
- Named a J.D. Power 2011 Customer Service Champion
- WGSN Global Fashion Awards "Outstanding Customer Service" and "Outstanding Etailer" 2010
- NRF Foundation / American Express Customers' Choice Awards Top 10 (2011 - #1; 2012 - #3)
- Recognition for Excellence in Customer Support and Service (RECSS) for Retail, 2009
- Shopzilla Circle of Excellence Platinum Award winner, 2004 – 2008 National Retail Federation "Top Ten in Customer Service" 2008
- Mobile Excellence Award Winner for Best User Experience, 2011[114]

How Zappos Does it

Zappos' success is a direct result of the company culture that they have developed. This culture is fiercely guarded to ensure that new hires are a fit and don't mess up the good thing that Zappos has going. Said another way, Zappos fiercely guards the gates, not any and every would-be employee can get in.

While Zappos is an online retailer of thousands of products and brands, their focus is really on customer service. Their mission is: "To provide the best customer service possible." It is believed that the fulfillment of that simple mission makes it possible for Zappos.com to

---

[114] (Zappos.com 2017; Michelli 2012)

Richard Solomon

successfully sell any collection and selection of products. To guide Zappos employees in achieving that mission, they have ten core values to direct them in their daily tasks:

1. *Deliver WOW Through Service*
2. *Embrace and Drive Change*
3. *Create Fun and A Little Weirdness*
4. *Be Adventurous, Creative, and Open-Minded*
5. *Pursue Growth and Learning*
6. *Build Open and Honest Relationships with Communication*
7. *Build a Positive Team and Family Spirit*
8. *Do More with Less*
9. *Be Passionate and Determined*
10. *Be Humble*[115]

These core values are way more than just nice phrases for marketing slogans or the company website; they use them as filters in hiring right. Let's take a deeper look at how Zappos hires right; how they make the values come alive and act as gatekeepers to the culture.

1. **"Scour the planet to find people who are fun and a little weird"**

Zappos understands that work need not be drudgery and heavy, so the company values fun and a bit of "weirdness" and knows that if this is to be maintained they have to find people who are, well ... "fun and a little weird."

---

[115] (Mickiewicz 2009)

Richard Solomon

When visitors go to the offices of Zappos in Henderson (now moved to Las Vegas), NV, they immediately realize that something is different about this place. Spaces are decorated with all kinds of pictures and quirky items that make the work areas a bit more light. It is not unusual to find staff playing odd games like laser tag or racing toy cars.

Once a year to show company spirit, employees are "encouraged" to shave their heads, paint/dye their hair blue, get a Mohawk or some other strange hairdo for the "weird hair day." And yes, the company brings the barbers and hairdressers to work!!!

2. **Look for technical skills but candidates must be a good cultural fit – must align to values**

Like Southwest Airlines, Zappos is clear that people need to fit into their way of doing things. Naturally they want technically sound people, but if they don't fit, then they don't get hired!!!!
Ever heard of a cultural interview? Well Zappos is very clear that if you want the company culture to be preserved and thrive, the people who get in the gate need to support and perpetuate it, not squelch it (isn't squelch a funny word?).
Questions in the interview are designed to see if candidates are a match and because the issues are not your normal run-of-the-mill ones, most candidates cannot rehearse an answer, thereby giving an authentic response. The second one is a trap because most candidates will not expect that weirdness and fun are actually what the company *is* looking for!!! Naturally

Richard Solomon

any hiring manager wants some variety in her team, but values are non-negotiable.

3. Conduct Multiple Interviews to Screen for Technical Skills and Values

Talking about interviews, imagine going to as many as eight (yes you read right) interviews!!! The aim here is that they want to be sure about the people they hire, so it was common in the early days of the company that a potential hire could have interviews with every member of a particular team. Naturally, this was not sustainable as the company grew, but at least they ensure candidates meet with a group from the people department (HR) and the functional or hiring manager, and some of their potential team members. Interestingly enough, functional managers have not resisted this – they actually had the opposite problem. It is simply that they all understand the importance of HIRING RIGHT.

This approach is in sharp contrast to some companies, where HR does the hiring using specs sent by the functional unit and weighs potentials such as technical ability, experience, and all that with very little (if any) attention paid to the so-called soft stuff, like culture fit, attitude, and emotional intelligence.

Zappos understands that the *soft* stuff *is* really the *hard stuff*, for it is infinitely easier to teach the technical skills. So they hire for fit and train for the rest.

Richard Solomon

4. Be Humble

Candidates (even would be executives) are often given a simple office chore by a very junior employee (this could be a hiring assistant) and their reaction gauged. If the response (body language included) is one that suggests that *this is below me, or this is way too simple for someone like me to do,* more than likely they won't get the job. Simple office chores could include filling in a mundane form, making photocopies or even a very basic Internet skills test. The idea here is simple, if your ego is too big, then you won't work out here.

5. Other Things Zappos Does in Hiring Right

a. Make the candidate as comfortable as possible – no high-pressure interviewing.

b. Even after being hired, if for some reason in the first few days it looks like a bad fit, you will be cut.

c. Managers spend 10–15 percent of their time socializing and building relationships.

d. Use crossword puzzles as part of the recruitment process to signal that this is a very different (and not so serious) place.

e. Use probes (questions, activities, behavioral interviews) to check for alignment between company values and recruit values.

Yes, I know you HR people are thinking that your "time to fill" metric will be royally screwed if you went this way, and depending on where in the world you recruit, some positions will be almost impossible to

Richard Solomon

fill. The same is true for Zappos, but they would rather do without that person than make a bad hiring decision; it simply costs more in the long run.

Zappos Will Pay You to Quit

Now here is a novel idea; Zappos will pay new recruits to quit, yes to quit!!! When new people are hired, everyone goes into training for four weeks, including culture training, customer service, and some operational work, usually on the switchboard as much of their service is delivered over the phone because there is no actual store to go to.

So new recruits start this four-week, deep immersion training where they learn the culture, service, values, and so on. (I know some of you must be thinking about your three-hour orientation workshop...) Anyway, at the start of week two, Zappos stops the training and says to the class: we would be happy to pay you for your time so far and top that off with a US$2,000.00 bonus no questions asked (if you choose to quit now)!!! Are you kidding me, who does that!!!??? Now as strange as this sounds, it actually makes perfect sense. The idea is to let those people who may have slipped through the net or have realized that this is simply not for them (anymore) walk out the door (as a matter of fact – to encourage it). The new hire gets a nice neat backdoor and a good bonus at that, and then Zappos saves itself the trouble of having to deal with someone who has other interests, or is just a misfit and will create more trouble than they are worth in the long-run to the organization.

It's essentially a bribe, ok an inducement, call it what you will; it's a great way to get rid of the round pegs that simply will not (or no longer) fit into the square holes (remember being a little weird is a

Richard Solomon

value) at Zappos. About ten percent of new recruits to the call center take them up on that deal, Zappos sees this as money well spent because they really want to fill the organization with the cream of the crop (as far as they define it). And would you believe it, turnover is low while satisfaction, engagement, and service quality is very high.[116]

What to Do

Here are some actions you can take from this chapter:

1. Hire for attitude – much of service delivery is about managing interactions.
2. Train for skill (see next chapter).
3. Find and retain the **<u>RIGHT</u>** people.
4. ID the real company values.
5. Put customer service high up on the values list.
6. Screen for culture fit.
7. Quality of hire is more important than time to fill.
8. It's better to leave a position empty a while longer than hire the wrong person.

Summary

"The Best Service Pros are just really great employees!!!" – *John Tschohl* – President, Service Quality Institute

To end this chapter and summarize, I start with a question: why would any company not try to hire willing, caring people who will go Above

---

[116] (McFarland 2008)

and Beyond the Call of Duty Every Time (hope you caught the *ABCDE*) to serve customers?

Ninety percent (90 percent) of service delivery normally rests in the hands of the front-liners. In fact, the people who have told us to hire for qualifications (above other factors) are wrong, especially in the customer-service domain. Even in highly technical areas, like aviation at Southwest Airlines, hire for attitude.

Think about it; the primary people resource needed to serve customers well is a positive attitude. The technical skills are important, but in the main can be quickly taught. Attitude on the other hand is very difficult – almost impossible — to change, unless the individual wants to and that desire itself is a facet of a positive attitude. Great efforts should go into finding and keeping the right people, and this reasoning holds for leaders too.

One of the problems with hiring is that, as companies grow, they tend to spread themselves out in an effort to get more warm bodies to do all the work that needs to be done. There is often some kind of compromise on the values and before you know it the company is losing its values (in practice) and the culture begins to slip.

For all those who are thinking: "Richard, these would be great in an ideal world, but in my company there is so much more to consider." Let me speak to you for a moment; I get that, I know, I have seen it; after two decades and hundreds of companies, I understand the pressure you are under. Here is what I know too: 85 percent of productivity comes from the interpersonal/attitude, versus the 15

Richard Solomon

percent that comes from technical skills according to several studies.[117]

You can go ahead and hire in desperation, but you will be just like so many organizations that call my office to solve a problem that was created on the day of hiring. The person was a poor selection from the start, but in a rush to fill the position, the organization simply settled and is now paying dearly for their mistake. Employees are much easier to hire than to fix or get rid of. It will always cost you more to deal with a poor hire than to find a great fit in the first place. Choose wisely.

---

[117] (Deutschendorf and Deutschendorf 2015)

Chapter 7

Orientation and Training

You ask: What if we train them and they leave? I ask: What if you don't train them and they stay? – Richard Solomon

Amazing Return on Investment (ROI)

One of the components of the **Signature Service Strategy** is training; you simply have to train and re-train your people. They need to be developed in alignment with what your organization wants to create, your very own service brand. I have heard people argue that the cost of training staff is too high, be cautious with this line of reasoning. If you can significantly reduce your customer defection rate and increase the levels of repeat business, I assure you that it will more than pay for the training. According to the Harvard Business Review, MBNA increased profits by 125 percent when it halved its rate of customer defection.[118] A study by the global business consulting firm Bain & Co. showed that a "5 percent increase in customer retention can increase a company's profitability by as much as 95 percent."[119]

---

[118] (Reichheld and W. Earl Sasser 1990)
[119] (Frederick Reichheld 2000)

Richard Solomon

So why do people doubt the value of training? I believe the problem here is that many leaders don't realize that return customers are where the sweet spot is; we already saw that they buy more than their new counterparts. Not only that, but it takes less work to sell to someone who has already bought from you. They know your company, your products and your service.

Here is an idea: why not divert some of the marketing or sales budget and create a retention budget (some of which can support training)? Now, now, now, don't get upset with me you marketing and sales people. I am in no way suggesting that marketing is unimportant or less important than service. In fact, it is vital, but once you get them in the door, someone has to treat them well or else the company becomes one big revolving door — a place where customers don't stay for any significant period and the company misses out on their lifetime value.[120] With the defection rate being such an epidemic, you have to admit that this may actually be a great idea. Citicorp conducted a study of 17 role model companies known for providing superior service. The study revealed that these service giants made investments of about 2 percent of gross sales in ongoing service education programs.[121]

Ok yes, I know you have employees who are qualified to do what they do, and they should be able to execute their functions well. But most people have worked in organizations that gave poor service, they have been customers who received poor service as well, and chances are they have themselves had lots of time to practice very bad

---

[120] *The value of a customer to an organization for the duration of their business relationship.*
[121] (Tschohl 2011)

Richard Solomon

customer-service habits. Add poor recruitment to this blend and you see the problem.

Habits are pesky little creatures. We all have them, and some can be helpful, like putting on your seatbelt before you start out on a road trip or locking the car as you walk away. But not all habits are useful. Most smokers seem to want to quit; many gamblers lose the shirts off their backs (the house never loses); and some people shop way more than their finances (or fiancées for that matter) are comfortable with (anyone say plastic?).

Even if you've done a great job at hiring the best people you could find, chances are they have built up some not-so-good service habits. But if your company is like most and has not had the good fortune of hiring right in the first place, this chapter becomes even more important for you, so read on.

The Anatomy of a Habit

The human brain is an amazing organ, and no supercomputer yet created can rival the ability of our brain to learn, analyze, or create. It is said that the most gifted geniuses only use a maximum of 10 percent of their brain power. Can you imagine what it would be like if someone got up to 50 percent? Wow! I wonder how much Dr. Sheldon Cooper – the fictional character played by Jim Parsons from the hit series *The Big Bang Theory* — uses?

In the movie *Limitless*, actor Bradley Cooper uses a fictional drug called NZT that somehow causes 80 percent of the human brain to be unlocked. He is instantly a genius, able to solve complex, long-standing problems with great ease... but I digress.

Richard Solomon

The human brain is constantly "remaking" itself, with cells dying and new ones being regenerated all the time. When we learn new things or make memories, the brain creates the equivalent of a "neurological circuit" that makes that item of learning easier to access in the future. The brain literally changes itself when we learn! You therefore become a different person because of learning.

When learning involves action-taking, the more we practice, the easier or more likely it is for us to take that action in the future. Think of all the things you do seemingly without effort or thought: using a smartphone, tying your shoes, and brushing your teeth all come to mind. Your brain now has a path of least resistance (a circuit) that makes doing these things easier than when you had just started.

A great example of this is driving. In the Caribbean, like many Commonwealth nations, we drive on the left side of the road; our cars are therefore right-hand-drive. If you live in the USA, Nigeria or China, then you drive on the right and you think we drive on the wrong side (FOR US LEFT IS RIGHT!!!). But when I travel and drive in a city where they drive on the other side, I have to remind myself to stay on the right. It is not that I forget as such; but more than once I have found myself dangerously turning onto the wrong side of a street, much to the ire of other drivers (these tourists!!!). I am aware of where I need to be, but because I have had almost 3 decades of practice doing it the other way, I sometimes revert to my neurological path of least resistance, unbeknownst to myself. If you have driven in a country where they drive on the "wrong side," then you have probably had a similar experience. Interestingly though, the more I drive on the right side, the less I am inclined to go to the left. *Maybe*

Richard Solomon

we can form new habits that are specific to certain conditions or geography, a geohabit?

Habits take even greater roots when we are rewarded in some way. This reward does not need to be overt, although this works too but the human body has its own reward mechanism. Shoppers, sex addicts, and gamblers alike get increased levels of dopamine[122] production in their brains when they engage in the desired activity. This powerful chemical affects the pleasure centers in the brain and causes the human to have a strong desire to repeat the action in the future, even if doing so is at their own peril.

What the Service Giants Do

One of the things that organizations that create customer loyalty do is orient (from the start) and train their people again and again to ensure they have the fundamentals in place and that the service message continues to sit high up in their minds. They also reward the right actions, making them more likely to be taken in the future. These companies don't leave it to chance; they go all out to make sure their people know what to do, know how to do it, and get reinforcement (we will look at this later on) for doing the right thing.

Having gone through the effort of finding the right people, they need to be oriented to our way of serving customers, what we stand for, our vision, what we value, and what service behaviors we see as useful, valuable, and necessary. They need to understand our history and why we see customers as we do. They must be indoctrinated in the

---

[122] A neurotransmitter produced in the brain linked to addiction, motivation, and rewards.

Richard Solomon

service culture we live. They need to drink the Kool Aid! We must ensure that they have the knowledge and skills to serve our customers as if they are all VIPs. Training must also extend to all leaders, managers, and supervisors; they need to learn how to lead and manage to support and propel customer loyalty.

Start Right and Send the Right Messages

A study by Citicorp found that training is most effective during an employee's early job experience with an organization.[123] It stands to reason that, when someone is new, eager, fresh, willing, flexible, pliable, motivated, it's the best time to impact them — get them early! Mix the Kool Aid extra strong... ok enough with the Kool Aid.

At the Ritz Carlton, new hires spend many days in orientation and training before they are *allowed* to serve customers.

St. Augustine wrote in a letter around 390CE, the Latin equivalent to "when in Rome, do as the Romans do." It is simply easier to fit in, and modern-day humans are no different. It's harder to go against the norm. You will find that coming into a strong, customer-focused culture will make it more likely that new employees will make a greater effort to give **signature** service consistently.

The Ritz sees itself as the varsity team, not some Saturday morning team that got together by chance or based on who happened to show up that morning (a "pick-up side" as we say in the Southern Caribbean). New recruits are given the very clear message that they are playing with the big boys now; this is not the minor league. They

---

[123] (Tschohl 2011)

Richard Solomon

are expected to perform at a level far above what they have done in the past. The Ritz wants the best – only the best.

Let's meet Suzy. Suzy will be our front-line (fictional) employee and since Suzy has been selected by The Ritz, she has already heard the mantra: "We are ladies and gentlemen serving ladies and gentlemen." This alone evokes images of well-dressed, well-mannered people serving deserving guests with a degree of professionalism and "quiet elegance" that has the efficient, yet serene image of VIP service (albeit quietly).

Here is the process that Suzy will be part of for the next year:

1. ***Orientation*** – *Suzy will have two days of new employee orientation where she will learn about company philosophy, history, and culture.*

2. ***Operational Certification*** - *Our Suzy will spend the next 21 days in training with an assigned learning coach who will train her on the skills and standards necessary to do her job successfully.*

3. *Next, Suzy will attend on **Day 21** a follow-up workshop to the orientation. This workshop is designed to ensure her engagement and success as she starts her journey with The Ritz-Carlton.*

4. ***All Aboard*** – *This "from Satisfaction to Engagement" workshop is designed to actively involve Suzy and all the ladies and gentlemen in identifying and developing the knowledge, skills, and*

Richard Solomon

abilities necessary to own and immediately resolve problems and opportunities.

5. ***The Radar On-Antenna Up*** *workshop is designed to actively involve Suzy in developing a new mind-set, skill-set, and tool-set for fulfilling not only the expressed, but also the unexpressed, wishes and needs of customers.*

6. *At **Day 180**, Suzy attends a training workshop designed to reconnect, review feedback, and update her personal action plan.*

7. ***Day 365*** *celebrates the first anniversary of Suzy's career with The Ritz-Carlton, and is an opportunity to re-energize the Gold Standards and culture.[124]*

That's a whopping 7 opportunities in the first year alone; almost one month of the first year of Suzy's employ at The Ritz Carlton is spent in training!!!

Additionally...

Suzy will continue to spend the first 15 – 20 minutes of every day in ongoing training. Yes, you read that right: EVERY SINGLE DAY!!! This is called the "Line Up," and during this time she will discuss with her co-workers and supervisor the Gold Standards,[125] how they can be and are being used:

---

[124] (Lampton, Ph. D 2003)
[125] (The Ritz-Carlton 2017)

1. **The Credo:** *"The Ritz-Carlton experience enlivens the senses, instills well-being, and fulfills even the unexpressed wishes and needs of our guests."*

2. **The three steps of service:**

   a. *Giving the guest a warm and sincere greeting (using the guest's name when possible).*

   b. *Anticipating and complying with guest needs.*

   c. *Saying a fond farewell, again using the guest's name.*

3. **Service Values: I Am Proud to Be Ritz-Carlton**

   a. *I build strong relationships and create Ritz-Carlton guests for life.*

   b. *I am always responsive to the expressed and unexpressed wishes and needs of our guests.*

   c. *I am empowered to create unique, memorable, and personal experiences for our guests.*

   d. *I understand my role in achieving the Key Success Factors, embracing Community Footprints and creating The Ritz-Carlton Mystique.*

   e. *I continuously seek opportunities to innovate and improve The Ritz-Carlton experience.*

   f. *I own and immediately resolve guest problems.*

   g. *I create a work environment of teamwork and lateral service so that the needs of our guests and each other are met.*

Richard Solomon

h. *I have the opportunity to continuously learn and grow.*

i. *I am involved in the planning of the work that affects me.*

j. *I am proud of my professional appearance, language, and behavior.*

k. *I protect the privacy and security of our guests, my fellow employees and the company's confidential information and assets.*

l. *I am responsible for uncompromising levels of cleanliness and creating a safe and accident-free environment[126].*

4. **The Employee promise:**

a. *At The Ritz-Carlton, our Ladies and Gentlemen are the most important resource in our service commitment to our guests.*

b. *By applying the principles of trust, honesty, respect, integrity, and commitment, we nurture and maximize talent to the benefit of each individual and the company.*

c. *The Ritz-Carlton fosters a work environment where diversity is valued, quality of life is enhanced, individual aspirations are fulfilled, and The Ritz-Carlton Mystique is strengthened.[127]*

---

[126] (The Ritz-Carlton 2017)
[127] *(The Ritz-Carlton 2017)*

Richard Solomon

5. The 20 Basics

a. The CREDO will be known, owned, and energized by all.

b. We are "Ladies and Gentlemen serving Ladies and Gentlemen."

c. The three steps of service shall be practiced by all employees.

d. "Smile" we are on stage. Always maintain positive eye contact.

e. Use the proper vocabulary with our guests. (Eliminate Hello, Hi, OK folks and No problem.)

f. Uncompromising levels of cleanliness are the responsibility of every employee.

g. Create a positive work environment. Practice teamwork and "lateral service."

h. Be an ambassador of your hotel in and outside of the work place. Always talk positive — No negative comments.

i. Any employee who receives a guest complaint "owns" the complaint.

j. All will ensure instant guest pacification. Respond to guest wishes within 10 minutes of the request. Follow up with a telephone call within 20 minutes to ensure their satisfaction.

k. Use guest incident forms to communicate guest problems to fellow employees and managers. This will help ensure that our guests are never forgotten.

l. Escort guests, rather than pointing out directions to another area of the hotel.

m. Be knowledgeable of hotel information (hours of operations, etc.) to answer guest inquires.

n. Use proper telephone etiquette. Answer within three rings and a "smile," ask permission to put a caller on hold. Do not screen calls. Eliminate call transfers when possible.

o. Always recommend the hotel's food and beverage outlets prior to outside facilities.

p. Uniforms are to be immaculate, wear proper footwear (clean and polished) and your correct nametag.

q. Ensure all employees know their roles during emergency situations and are aware of procedures. (Practice fire and safety procedures monthly.)

r. Notify your supervisor immediately of hazards, injuries, equipment or assistance needs you have.

s. Practice energy conservation and proper maintenance and repair of hotel property and equipment.

t. Protecting the assets of a Ritz-Carlson Hotel is the responsibility of every employee.[128]

---

[128] (The Ritz-Carlton 2017)

Richard Solomon

The Ritz Gets It

The Ritz gets it; they know that the process of ongoing training and focus is at the heart of its legendary **signature** service. It is because of the quality of staff, the ongoing training, and the culture it has created that they will continue to have stories like the ones below.

> *"Enrique, a bellhop, noticed that a lady customer was having difficulty shutting her suitcase – he tried to help, but in fact the catches were broken and there was no way to secure the suitcase. The guest was due to leave shortly and there was no time to go to the mall to buy a replacement. Shortly after, Enrique went off duty, but he continued to be concerned about the guest. He went home, took a suitcase he had recently bought for a holiday from his wardrobe and returned immediately to the hotel to give it to the guest."*[129]

> *"One family staying at the Ritz-Carlton, Bali, had carried specialized eggs and milk for their son who suffered from food allergies. Upon arrival, they saw that the eggs had broken and the milk had soured. The Ritz-Carlton manager and dining staff searched the town but could not find the appropriate items. But the executive chef at this particular resort remembered a store in Singapore that sold them. He contacted his mother-in-law, and asked that she buy the products and fly to Bali to deliver them, which she agreed to do. Of course the family was delighted. After an experience like that, do you think this particular family would even consider staying somewhere else?"*[130]

---

[129] (Farrance 2002)
[130] (Help Scout 2017)

Richard Solomon

Often these stories are told during the morning "line-up," doing this provides a number of valuable benefits:

1. It keeps legendary service top-of-mind for all employees.
2. It says to employees that it's ok to bend the rules to keep customers happy.
3. It rewards employees for rule-bending in favor of the customer's comfort.
4. Employees get local fame from being recognized in front of their peers.
5. It gives others ideas about how they can use the gold standards.

Putting on the Ritz

The ladies and gentlemen at the Ritz create mystique by paying close attention to all guests and sensibly anticipating their every need. What appears to happen as if by magic is really thoughtfulness, care and deep consideration for all guests. Mystique is also a computer program in which Ladies and Gentlemen enter guest preferences, which are then available at all Ritz hotels so that the next time you stay at a Ritz hotel, they will know exactly how you like your coffee, which paper you like, whether to leave an aromatherapy candle in your room or how you prefer your eggs.

Baptism in the Street

In Port-of-Spain Trinidad, a Hyatt Regency hotel opened opposite the Crowne Plaza (turned Radisson) in January 2008 – literally across the street. Locals mostly staff the Hyatt Port-of-Spain, so I believe it is safe to assume that these same people previously worked at other hotels on the island (including the Crowne Plaza I suspect). It would also be safe to assume that given the bland service which tends to obtain in so many organizations, some of the same employees would have been part of lackluster service provision elsewhere. How then does the Hyatt manage to deliver possibly the best customer service among hotels on the island? Were the employees baptized in the middle of the street? How is it that their behavior changed on the other side? This definitely was not achieved by accident; Hyatt must be very deliberate in its efforts at recruitment, orientation, training, and measurement.

"But Richard, we already have all our staff – we don't get to start over!" I know some of you must be thinking about this; what do you do, you don't have the luxury of a startup that can hire right the first time, nor can you get rid of everyone and start anew. I know you must be smiling at that thought, but no you can't do it, sorry. People feel that way all the time, "if only we could start over..."

Basically, there are a handful of things (or a little more) you can do in this situation:

1. Get your service vision and message clear.
2. Start hiring right immediately – make sure everyone who comes in the door from now on fits the employee attitude profile as much as possible.
3. Train and train and train the ones that are already hired.
4. Measure performance – find a way to measure service delivery down to the individual level.
5. Continue to train, coach, and send the right messages.

Richard Solomon

6. Reassign people who may not be a good fit but have other strengths

7. Get rid of the people who don't improve over the medium term (yes you read that right – get rid of them!). Are you serious or not?

8. Hold all leaders accountable for promoting, modeling and leading for **signature** service.

Learn to Respond to Customers' Complaints

When customers complain, it's hardly because they just want to be a pain in the (you know where). Instead, it is normally something about your product, process, system, or more so, about your people that is causing the ire. Usually customers respond strongest to fairness failures; that is, where they believe they have been treated unfairly. According to researcher Kathleen Seiders from Babson College, Massachusetts, in these cases, their reactions are generally immediate, emotional, and enduring. Systems aren't unfair, nor do they treat people unfairly; people are and do.

Whether the issue is unfairness or some other matter that the customer deems a problem, the key issue is knowing how to respond. Ongoing training is so indispensable here, and it does not matter if you don't agree with the customer or believe they don't have a good enough reason to complain. The fact is that they are unhappy about something that has to do with your organization and it is in your best interest to fix it.

Richard Solomon

When it comes to fixing service failures, some moves and actions go farther than others; here are a few tips that go a long way in the face of customer complaints:

1. **Self-First**: The service professional must remain calm, avoid becoming defensive, and show poise. Self-control is actually the foundation of responding to customer complaints.

2. **Deal with their Emotions**: Let the customer vent, listen, show understanding and empathy, and practice humility.

3. **Apologize**: Give a genuine apology for what has transpired and their troubles. It does not matter if it was the fault of your functional area or not; their troubles and upset are enough to warrant a genuine apology. *"I am so sorry this is affecting you, if it were me I would be upset too."*

4. **Fix it Quickly**: Once they have vented, tell them what you are going to do to make it right and go into action quickly. Maybe this will cost the organization a few dollars. Trust me, in the face of the customer lifetime value and the bad publicity that can result, you should spend the few dollars to make things right.

5. **Don't Quote Policy**: Customers **HATE, hate, hate** it when people quote company policy to them and they hate it even more when policies are the response to a complaint. Don't even mention the word policy; quoting policy has two effects, **firstly** it gives the appearance you are hiding behind the rules so as not to fix the issue; **secondly** it says to the customer: "your request is unreasonable or ridiculous." If you must, then bend the rules or find someone who can!

Richard Solomon

6. **Make It Up to Them**: On top of fixing whatever the issue was, quickly find a way to make it up to them. What can you do to sweeten the pot so much that the problem is no longer the focus? Give a discount, throw in a freebie, what about complimentary service for a certain period or waiving the charge all together? [131]

Every day, your organization has opportunities to fix situations where customers are unhappy. Remember 70 percent of complaining customers will do business with you again if you resolve the complaint in their favor; that number jumps to 95 percent if you resolve the issue on the spot.[132] In case you are wondering about the customers who only complain to get something for nothing, fear not, they are in the minority (around 3 percent).

Naturally, systems must be designed so that they back up the above approaches to mend the customer relationships. Take the position of "let's sort this out," and certainly don't become antagonistic or annoyed; never pick a fight with a customer, for it is one that you are bound to lose. **Don't fight, make it right!!!**

In addition to training your people on the transactional and technical elements of the job, be sure to train them on the people side of dealing with customer complaints. When a customer believes that they are being shortchanged, taken advantage of, or treated unfairly, these humans get upset or angry.

The human brain is actually three different "brains." The **first** is the primitive brain, brain stem or lizard brain; it is called the lizard

---

[131] (Zemke and Bell 2000)
[132] (LeBoeuf 2000)

Richard Solomon

brain because lizards have the same brain structure. This is concerned with safety, security, survival, and reproduction. The **second** is the limbic system or emotional brain, and it is also referred to as the mammalian brain, as other mammals also have this. This part of the brain is concerned with relationships, processing emotions, and producing a variety of chemicals including dopamine, endorphins, and serotonin. The **third** "brain" is the neocortex or the new brain. It is responsible for analysis, logic, and what we traditionally term intelligence.[133]

When we get upset or angry, it is almost impossible to be clear and rational. Blood flow to our neocortex falls and increases to the limbic system and lizard brain. If people feel threatened, then it is even worse because the primitive brain becomes more active. The limbic system produces higher amounts of adrenaline and cortisol; less oxytocin is produced, which makes it difficult to regulate emotions. In essence, people are less reasonable and logical but are more emotional and given to flight or fight.

No, you do not need a degree in psychology or neuroscience to successfully deal with angry or upset customers, but understanding how they (we) react internally and being emotionally intelligent certainly helps. Everyone needs to be trained in how to deal with customers — angry or not. This is a sure way to turbo boost your company's service delivery.

One note of caution, training is not just for dealing with angry or upset customers. I highlight this here because it is a powerful example of why training is important for all your people. In addition, your

---

[133] *(MacLean 1990)*

Richard Solomon

people need what I will call "**Signature** Service training" to treat all customers like VIPs.

Train the Middle

Training should not just be provided for general staff and those who serve customers directly. It must also be for those who manage and lead them. Remember, it is the middle that has ongoing contact with the frontline, and it is also the middle that has to oversee the execution of strategies, the facilitation of empowerment, and the general approach to managing people is in their hands.

One supermarket decided to train the store associates in various customer-service techniques, but they neglected to train store managers. One of the techniques store associates learned was the 8-foot rule; simply, the rule guides store associates to acknowledge a customer, greet them and offer help once they come within an 8-foot radius of the associate. Associates are required to be aware of the customers around them and take action when necessary; naturally this took staff away from other store duties from time to time.

On one occasion, a supervisor was annoyed that an associate was taking too long to complete the replenishing of a shelf. When the staffer explained the 8-foot rule as the reason, he was reprimanded and told that they (the store) had sales targets and could not meet the targets if the shelves were empty. The supervisor went to on to scold that he had no time for "head office dreams." From this example, managers have (in the past) learned the importance of keeping stock on the shelves and the negative impact of stock-outs on sales targets. Keeping the shelves stocked and the register ringing might be their mantra, but it takes more than filled shelves to keep customers happy. Whatever your people are trained to do, their managers must be trained to facilitate, encourage, reward, and uphold. If the front line is trained to operate a particular way and managers are not indoctrinated in the same approaches and provided tools on how to support it, once people get back to their home locations or everyday work they will follow the dictates of their leaders. The organization needs to be in alignment, because misalignment causes frustration, inefficiency, and unnecessary costs.

Signature Service Training

Training programs and courses are a dime a dozen, and maybe you have your own training department or a favorite provider. When my firm provides training to client organizations, we generally go through a full cycle of first assessing the needs, then designing the training (including knowledge and skill acquisition), followed by delivering the training, we facilitate in building the supports and identifying the barriers, planning for implementation, monitoring execution, and finally measuring the results.

That process could easily fill another book; there are lots of good resources available on the topic of developing and delivering training. One very good one is *Telling Ain't Training* by Stolovitch and Keeps. This section is not intended to teach training design and delivery, however, but more so to give a high-level view of some of the important training content to include in your **signature** service training initiative.

Richard Solomon

For the Front Line

1. The Service Environment	2. The Signature Service Vision
a. Competition b. Customers' expectations c. Profile of the 21st century customer d. Economic realities e. Making the business case for **signature** service	a. What is **signature** service? b. What it means to us c. Making all customers feel like VIPs d. Our service standards
3. Self as a Service Tool	**4. Customer Interactions**

a. Emotional Intelligence
b. Attitude toward service
c. Feeling good about yourself
d. Using your circle of Influence
e. ABCDE – Above and Beyond the Call of Duty Every time
	a. VIP expectations
	b. Positive communication
	c. Using body language
	d. Words and phrases to avoid
	e. Words and phrases to embrace
	f. Responsiveness
	g. Our special/branded interaction process (see APPLE example below)
	  i. **A** - Approach customers with a personalized, warm welcome.
	  ii. **P** - Probe politely to understand all the customer's needs.

Richard Solomon

5. Taking Ownership for Signature Service
 	
    a. This is your customer
    b. Taking ownership of the customer needs
    c. Completing the service cycle
    d. Concierge thinking
	iii. **P** - Present a solution for the customer to take home today.
	iv. **L** - Listen for and resolve any issues or concerns.
	v. **E** - End with a fond farewell and an invitation to return.[134]

6. Customer Transactions
 	
    a. VIP expectations
    b. Speed and accuracy
    c. Being technically strong/understanding and using systems
    d. A model for transaction efficiency
    e. Delivery and follow-up
	7. Empowerment
	
	    a. What is empowerment
	    b. Barriers to empowerment
	    c. Overcoming the barriers
	    d. Service opportunities to use your empowerment
	    e. Receiving and taking empowerment

[134] (Gallo 2012)

8. Maintaining Signature Service	9. When Things go Wrong
a. Co-workers are customers too b. Teaming up to provide **signature** service c. Forever focus on service	a. The emotional side of service problems b. Steps to service recovery/a service recovery model c. Solving service problems quickly d. Don't fight – make it right e. Handling your most challenging customers

Richard Solomon

For the Leaders of the Front line

1. **The Service Environment**	2. **The Signature Service Vision**
a. Competition b. Customers' expectations c. Profile of the 21st century customer d. Economic realities e. Making the business case for **signature** service	a. What is signature service? b. What **signature** service means to us c. Making all customers feel like VIPs d. Our service standards
3. **Designing the Signature Customer Experience**	4. **Empowerment**
a. Mapping the customer experience b. Measuring the customer experience c. Making changes to the process	a. What is empowerment? b. Barriers to empowerment c. Overcoming the barriers d. Giving away your power
5. **Leading for Signature Service**	6. **Motivation Skills for Service Leaders**
a. Self as a leadership tool b. What do **signature** service leaders do? c. Leading by example d. Holding the vision e. Coaching for **signature** service	a. What is motivation? b. What motivates your people c. The vision as a motivator d. Daily motivating actions

Richard Solomon

7. Communication	8. Maintaining Signature Service
a. Importance of communication in leading others b. Body language c. The communication funnel d. Language that helps and language that hurts	a. Internal service b. Building your service team c. Recognition and rewards d. **Signature** service – a daily focus

Naturally these outlines are pretty generic and only intended as examples. Your situation may require something different and your customer experience map (see chapter 9) may call for added components or changes. There may be specific gaps that need to be filled or industry-specific add-ons, like the 8-foot rule in a supermarket, or the host/hostess in the restaurant industry. Whatever you do, be sure to build a robust program that covers the crucial points. And remember that training is but one part of the formula.

Making Training Stick

Training is only part of the formula used to create **signature** service, but it's a very important part. When we train employees or managers, we seek to impart knowledge, build skills, and to some extent, change attitudes. Training should never be done in a vacuum, it is either you want to fill a gap that currently exists, or you want to prepare for something to come.

Richard Solomon

Let's say, for example, that in making your business case you realized that only 20 percent of customer complaints are solved on the spot in the customers' favor. Remember, 95 percent of complaining customers will do business with you again if you resolve the complaint in their favor on the spot. On further examination, you find that another 40 percent end in no resolution and the remaining 40 percent are referred to a supervisor or manager. The gap here would likely be one of empowerment; training could be one of the solutions along with coaching and changing authority levels. This is therefore specific, you would not just be doing "training," that would be like going to a pharmacy and asking for "medicine." Instead, you would have training delivered that is specific to the need identified. Too many times I get calls and emails from clients who want generic "customer service" training instead of identifying the specific gap to be closed.

You could spend millions on training courses and receive very little return on your investment or return on expectations, if what participants learn is not transferred to the workplace. [135] The transference of learning continues to be a real challenge; yet without training, your whole **signature** service strategy would be undermined. Over the years through my client work, I have identified certain tactics that make training stick and greatly increase the rate of transference back to work.

Manager support

Support from the line manager or supervisor is extremely important, this actually starts before the training begins. Managers and staff need to be clear on the gap to be filled and what is expected when people

---

[135] (Reichheld and W. Earl Sasser 1990)

Richard Solomon

return from training. Once the training is done (or during in the case of an extended program), managers must make it ok, and encourage the application of the learning. Have them come up with an application plan that might include the why, who, what, where, when, and how learnings can be applied, plus any additional support they may need. Follow-up on the implementation of plans and monitor application on a regular basis.

Additionally, a great way to support trainees is by having them teach others what they learned. This may be in the form of a simple presentation, maybe a lunch-and-learn where people bring their lunch (or it can be provided) and have a presentation plus a discussion. Have the group agree on an application plan and let the team do its work with the support of managers.

Competent training

Training needs to be well-designed, meet needs and well-delivered. The knowledge that people gain should have immediate applicability and they should enjoy the training experience. Find trainers who can connect with your people and deliver clear, useful training experiences.

Training should also appeal to the five different learning styles. Some learners are more **visual**, they learn well by seeing information and visualizing concepts; use charts, infographics, presentations, and video to appeal to them. **Auditory** learners learn best by hearing, talking out loud, video, listening to information, asking and answering questions also work well with this group. Learners with a preference for **reading and writing** love to interact with text, quizzes, and handouts. Written case studies and stories are helpful too. Lastly, we

Richard Solomon

have **kinesthetic** learners who essentially learn best by doing. Demonstrations, exercises, role-plays and moving around help these learners. Infographic 34 shows the four learning styles.

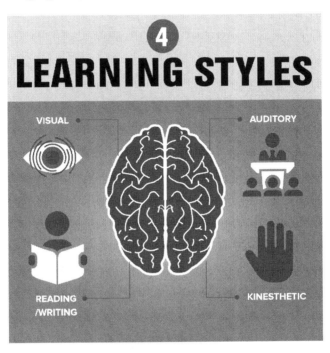

Infographic 34

Of course, you never have a class of full of any one type of learner, and most people have at least two styles that dominate the others. A good strategy is to ensure that any training you do or that is done appeals to all four learning styles.

I have found that delivering training over an extended period can be useful both in terms of opportunities to apply the learning and less interruption of the business. The mixing of delivery modes can be excellent as well; some courses or modules can be face-to-face and others done by video, e-learning, peer-to-peer teaching, or on-the-job exercises. A recent study indicated that in-person, instructor-led training is still the most used and most effective, with e-learning following closely behind. See table 4 for the ranking of even more training modalities.

Competency Based Training and Assessment

A competency is defined as *a measurable pattern of knowledge, skills, abilities, behaviours, and other characteristics that an individual needs to perform work roles or occupational functions successfully.*[136]

Ultimately, you need to be sure that your people possess the ability to perform the tasks that make up their job roles. The design of training must seek to impart the knowledge, build the skills and hone the behaviors and characteristics for **signature** service delivery. We must not only train employees, we must be sure that they are actually competent and able to do the work.

Employees must be certifiable in terms of the competencies required by their roles. This may involve various types of assessment including but not limited to: observation, case studies, role-plays, psychometric and aptitude tests. All categories of employees must be included as everyone serves someone either insider or outside the organization and impacts the strategy. Unlike what is regularly done, this goes past the reaction assessment used at the close of a training workshop or the "happy sheet" (as I often call it), and involves the actual measurement of learning, behaviour and business results.[137]

---

[136] (Rodriguez et al. 2002)
[137] (Kirkpatrick and Kirkpatrick 2010)

Richard Solomon

TRAINING MODALITIES, 5-POINT SCALE FOR USE AND EFFECTIVENESS		
MODALITY	**USE**	**EFFECTIVENESS**
In-person, instructor-led classroom	3.40	3.79
eLearning modules	2.78	3.23
Informal peer-to-peer learning	2.59	3.56
On-the-job exercises	2.58	3.71
Coaching/mentoring	2.48	3.88
Paper-based performance support	2.43	2.85
Online performance support	2.33	3.23
Conference calls	2.28	2.53
Video learning	2.17	2.95
Virtual synchronous classroom	2.13	3.00
Industry conferences/events	2.07	2.82
Pre-recorded instructor led training	2.03	2.56
Recorded Webinars	2.01	2.51
Published books or research	1.83	2.37
Social/collaboration tools	1.83	2.98
Mobile Learning delivery	1.70	2.86
On-line academic institutions	1.69	2.70
In-person academic institutions	1.68	2.95
Games/simulations (in-person)	1.52	3.00
Games/simulations (online)	1.48	2.83
Podcasts	1.45	2.39

Table 4[138]

---

[138](Freifeld 2016)

Finding an application that keeps the service focus alive between training sessions is a nice added touch. WhatsApp, private Facebook groups, and applications like Slack are all possibilities here. Keep in mind that someone has to administer the groups and keep the conversations primed and alive.

Application Opportunity

"To know and not to do is not to know." - Chinese proverb

One of the best ways to help training stick is to ensure that learners have opportunities to apply their learning. Once they get back on the job, you want to make sure they can quickly begin to apply their newfound knowledge and skills. Don't leave this to chance, as said before, managers and supervisors need to facilitate this. The sooner after training they apply what they learn, the more likely it will stick for the longer term and become part of "the way we work."

Company culture

If the company is one that encourages learning and application, and rewards and recognizes those who learn and improve performance as a result of their application, there is a much greater likelihood that people will want to learn and apply and hence make learning stick. Learning organizations facilitate ongoing learning and development among its people in service of continuously improving. They place a high value on this and recognize it as a critical part of their success formula. A company culture that values service and learning to support the delivery of **signature** service to customers will encourage

Richard Solomon

learners to acquire new knowledge and skill and apply them. Chapter 10 covers culture and culture re-engineering in much greater detail.

Continuous training

Some people (leaders in particular) believe that you could train people once for a day or two and then it's over, the people should somehow know and do well after the annual or bi-annual event. **THIS DOES NOT WORK!!!!** I know of no profession where people are expected to perform and grow without ongoing learning. The best service companies in the world make training a normal part of their organization. Remember Michael from South African Airways? He said that every month they are in some kind of service training. Suzy from The Ritz Carlton spent almost one month of the first year in training, plus her morning line up and continued on-the-job training. Zappos employees are in "deep immersion" training for four full weeks to start with; at Disney the training never stops; and Apple geniuses go to Cupertino, California for two weeks of training and continue learning throughout the time they spend at the tech giant.

In my experience, to many organizations, training is a task to be completed: training done, box ticked; not recognizing that **signature** service will not come as a result of a one-off or annual training event. The two most usual complaints I hear are that the operations are interrupted and cost. Don't let these be excuses, you need to keep the engine tuned to improve performance, the Formula 1 driver can't be so concerned about the race that he refuses to make a pit stop. In terms of cost, sure it needs to be managed but the resulting improved service will more than pay for itself as we saw in chapter 2, plus you can develop internal resources (trainers) to deliver ongoing training.

Richard Solomon

Remember that service leaders spend around 2 percent of gross sales on ongoing service related education.[139]

Orientation and Training is Not Enough

Hiring the right people with the right attitude to work is critical, and orienting and training them is also crucial. But how employees are treated or engaged on an ongoing basis by the organization is just as important. It stands to reason that, if organizations are unfair, unreasonable, or display any such negatives toward employees regularly, the employees are less likely to serve customers well. In our own experience, when employees feel that the organization cares for them, they in turn are more inclined to go above and beyond the call of duty and give the discretionary effort to make the customer experience truly **signature**.

A recent article in *Global Business and Organizational Excellence* cited extensive research that proves the clear link between engagement and customer-centricity at DHL.[140] Towers and Perrin 2003; Haid & Sims, 2009; Harter et al., 2009, and Gonring, 2008, have all proven a similar link, but isn't it obvious? In short, organizations must take care of the foundational elements of employee engagement and make direct efforts to ensure the higher-order factors are in place to assure maximum engagement. Foundational elements include: reasonable/fair pay, good working conditions, security, proper supervision/management, ethical decision-making, and the like. Higher-order factors include:

---

[139] (Tschohl 2011)
[140] (MacGillavry and Sinyan 2016)

Richard Solomon

empowerment, room for personal growth, recognition, advancement, and achievement.

Internal Service

Think with me for a moment: is it reasonable to expect that your people will serve the customers with joy and enthusiasm if they themselves are not served well internally? No right-thinking person could answer yes to this question, yet many organizations allow their people to be treated with disregard and disrespect by internal servers and yet expect joyful service to the customer. This is illogical thinking at least, and oxymoronic at worst. Organizations are whole systems, one cannot expect to have unhappiness and disrespect in one quarter and have happiness and respect in another. Of course the organization will be busy at times, and all resources won't always be available, employees should not expect perfection. However, when managers (for example) are allowed to treat staff as **things,** disempower them, embarrass them, disregard them and the like, we cannot expect better treatment to be extended to our customers. The connection to leadership is clear and should not be overlooked.

What to do

1. Get your service vision clear.
2. Build an employee attitude profile.
3. Hire for attitude and train for skill.
4. Orient new employees within days of taking up their position (mix the Kool aid extra strong).
5. Engage employees at multiple levels.
6. Design and deliver great service trainings

7. Train, train, and train again.

8. Make sure leaders promote and model the service message.

9. Include emotional intelligence and interpersonal skills training for all front-liners and also instruct on how to deal with upset customers.

10. Ensure internal service is stellar

Summary

Here is the conclusion of the matter; I am going to make this easy and to the point. You want your company to provide **signature** service to your customers, then you must find the best people, orient them, train them, coach them, monitor them, keep training them at all levels, and don't leave it to chance. Make sure they are skilled in service delivery and they remain sharp through ongoing training and opportunities to apply.

Richard Solomon

Chapter 8

Empowerment

"There can be no signature service without empowerment."

– Richard Solomon

Five Monkeys and a Banana

Five monkeys were placed in a cage with a nice ripe, yellow banana hanging from the top and a ladder placed conveniently under the waiting treat. Naturally, one of the primates quickly begins to climb the ladder, expecting an easy payoff; no sooner had he hit the first rung then all the other monkeys were sprayed with ice cold water. He quickly recedes to the far corner, seeing the onslaught on his cage-mates. After a very short while, another monkey cautiously follows, and the others are again sprayed with the ice water. Another tries, finding it hard to resist the temptation, but sadly his cage-mates meet the same uncomfortable fate. After a while, these five monkeys are sitting looking at the banana hanging *right there* but beyond their reach. If one of them makes a move to try, the others quickly set upon him with fists of fury; they are trying to prevent not so much him from getting the banana but more so themselves from getting sprayed.

The researcher (torturer is more like it) puts away the hose; removes one of the monkeys and replaces it with a "fresh" one who has never had the ice water experience. No sooner is he in the cage then he sees the banana and you guessed it, starts climbing the steps. What do you think happens? To the new guy's surprise and horror, the four other (more experienced) monkeys begin to attack him. He learns the lesson very quickly: "try to climb the stairs and get assaulted."

Next, the researcher removes yet another of the original five monkeys and replaces it with a new one. The newcomer goes to the stairs and is attacked. The previous newcomer takes part in the punishment with enthusiasm! Likewise, replace a third original monkey with a new one, then a fourth, then the fifth. Every time the newest monkey takes to the stairs, it is attacked. Most of the monkeys now delivering the beating have no idea why they were not permitted to climb the stairs, or why they are participating in the beating of the newest monkey.

After replacing all the original monkeys, none of these remaining monkeys have ever been sprayed with cold water; nevertheless, no monkey ever again approaches the stairs to try for the banana. Note that all the monkeys *now* in the cage are new and don't know why they beat each other for going for an obviously easy treat, but they know "that's the way it's done around here."

Does any of this look familiar? Someone tries to do what seems right or sensible and gets chewed out for it by "the organization?" This happens a few times and before you know it everyone is overly careful and the stories of "ice water" get passed along the grapevine. Before too long, employees are hiding behind weak phrases like "that's the policy" and "no sir we cannot do that – it's against our operational manual," or "my supervisor would have to approve that and they are not around."

If you remember before, we talked about service points and flash points as being opportunities to serve the customer, and while we can plan for service points, flash points are harder to plan for. These are crucial times when your people have to think and act, and how they act will be in part determined by how empowered they are.

Managers and leaders cannot think, act, and learn for the entire company; we need the wider skill and commitment of the whole. Your people should be given Standard Operating Practices as to what should be done in most service situations or at service points. But they should not be straight-jacketed into only those approaches alone.

Think with me: If we hire right, orient, and train, most of our staff will understand what we are working toward. Given the power to think and act, they will do so in the way we need them to. In circumstances where they don't, we can coach, train, and develop; if these fail and keep failing over the medium term, we move them around or even out. Freeing your people to think and act, even bend the green rules (rules that can be bent under the appropriate circumstances), will mean that you believe them to be intelligent and have the best interest of your customers and the company at heart.

Where is the Power at CAL?

Like most airlines, at Caribbean Airlines Limited, the name on the travel document must match the name on the booking. On a family trip, the first and middle names on my elder daughter's ticket were switched; not having made the booking myself, I had no idea how this

Richard Solomon

happened. With our check-in on pause, I was blandly informed that I would have to pay about US$30 to have the change made. I asked why should I pay for such a simple transaction. The robotic answer coming from the counter agent was "that's the policy." I looked at her and simply said can't you make an empowered decision to waive the fee? She said that she did not have the authority to do it and the policy was clear. My next question seemed to throw her for a loop; why does such a policy exist, I simply enquired as I failed to see the logic for this. The twenty-something year old had no idea. Imagine that, you work for a company, you know the rules, you are instructed to quickly whip customers with them, but you have no idea why they exist!!!???

The supervisor I spoke to next was only slightly more knowledgeable (but just as unhelpful), as she explained the security risks involved in allowing passengers to travel with even slight name differences on documents. This I accepted, but I asked, "seeing that you can see this is clearly not a security breach but human error, can't you make the change without the charge?" (I was pushing her limits of empowerment). She resisted my press and said that someone above her could do it, but he was on lunch and again told me that I had to pay the charge. I pushed even more and she disappeared into the back office, only to emerge a few minutes later with the same answer (from that unseen lunching "someone"). I grudgingly paid the $30 and proceeded on my journey.

I am trained to see what lies beneath the surface and here is what I saw:

1. The "supervisor" did not have the power to make **a $30 decision!!!**

Richard Solomon

2. The more senior person did not have enough faith in their staff to empower them to make basic decisions that deviate from the letter of the policy. They sat in the back office and simply relegated her to the rank of messenger, instead of taking advantage of the asset of a living breathing employee and allowing her to make a simple yet customer-pleasing decision.

3. The agent at the gate had no idea **why** the rule existed.

4. I saw a little empathy from CAL's staff, but they did not have enough latitude or bravery to bend a clearly green rule[141] to make the customer happy.

5. And while not beneath the surface - *a 30-second, thirty-dollar decision could have earned them a little praise in this book.*

Here, the annoyance is not the fee itself but the inflexibility, and that it is more of a nuisance charge. What many companies don't realize is that these little (seemingly insignificant) decisions leave an indelible impression on the customer, either encouraging him to come again or spend his money elsewhere.

Not Much Better at the Sheraton

I sometimes wonder if I do something to attract these experiences. It may just be that given what I do, it is hard not to notice these issues. I am also loath to tolerate substandard service without pushing for better, or as my children like to say, "complaining bitterly!"

So we signed up for one of those resort tours at a Sheraton resort in Orlando; the documentation asked us to bring two forms of ID

---

[141] *A green rule is one that can be bent to please or satisfy a customer; it breaks no laws, nor does it compromise safety or any principles.*

Richard Solomon

(including our passport) to the 10:30 a.m. appointment. After driving through pre-Isaac[142] rain and the resulting traffic to get there, we were asked for our ID; I presented my driver's license and my national ID (very much like a Social Security Card). I was told that I needed my passport (which I honestly forgot) to go on this tour (now remember, they invited us!). I told the rep that I did not have my passport and there was no way I would go back to my villa to get it in this weather. Incredulously, she told me that, if I did not have the travel document, I could not go on the tour (that they wanted to take me on to promote *their* services!!!).

Now here is where the story gets crazy. A manager of something or the other comes over and politely shows me the line in the documentation that said I should have my passport. Yes, I know what the documentation says, and yes, I forgot it. But why do you need it? I have with me two other forms of government-issued ID. This man with a badge that said "Manager" simply said "this is what we require." Are you kidding me?! Being the pesky customer that I am, I said: I know it is what you require; my question is WHY!!! The bottom line was he did not know why and could not bend the almighty rule to save me time and, more importantly, promote their product to a potential customer. I wonder how much business they lost as a result? No one will ever know.

Sadly, stories like these are repeated every day around the globe; employees boxed in by all-important, unbendable rules or too afraid to color outside the lines — sad, very sad.

---

[142] Hurricane Isaac 2012

Richard Solomon

Even the US Congress is Taking Notice

Sometimes a lack of empowerment can have catastrophic consequences. In chapter 5, I referred to the situation where United Airlines had Dr. David Dao dragged bloodied off flight United 3411 on April 9, 2017.[143] Their stock price took a huge hit and they settled the lawsuit for an undisclosed sum.[144] As if the bad publicity and scenes of customers destroying their frequent flyer cards were not enough; the event seemed to trigger a US Congress enquiry.

The airlines represented were Alaska, American, Southwest and United Airlines, with Delta Airlines declining to testify, stating that they were already in talks with individual members of congress about improving customer service.

House Transportation and Infrastructure Committee, chairman Bill Shuster led the hearing. Unsurprisingly, Southwest was way out front of the rest, being able to identify many customer friendly policies and amazing empowerment of the line staff.

Needless to say, United was the one over the barrel although American took quite a bruising. Members of congress relayed their own experiences and those of their constituents. Congressman Rodney Davis had actually conducted a survey of two thousand plus of his constituents to prepare for the hearing. Again, it was praise for Southwest and a whipping for the rest. In his testimony a visibly uncomfortable United CEO Oscar Munoz regularly deferred to Kerry Philipovitch, the airline's senior vice president of customer experience, who in my opinion should have resigned given all the

---

[143] (Mindock 2017)
[144] (Udland 2017)

Richard Solomon

customer debacles that United has found itself in in recent times. To be fair, he (Munoz) did say that ultimately he is responsible and listed the four main failures that resulted in the Dr. Dao debacle:

1. Calling on law enforcement when there was neither a safety nor security problem

2. Rebooking crew at the very last minute – creating an unnecessary challenge

3. Not offering a high enough incentive or compensation for customers to give up their seat

4. And finally: *"...perhaps the largest failure, our employees **did not have the authority** to do what was right, or to use frankly their commonsense..."*[145]

There it is, a direct quote from the horse's mouth, the reason this billion dollar mess occurred is mainly because United's staff did not have the power to do the right thing!

American Airlines particularly gave many politically correct responses, painting a picture that we passengers are yet to see. To the trained ear, their answers revealed several glaring holes in customer-focused training efforts and empowerment. Congress chided the airlines for the general mishandling of customers and burying their (customers') rights deep within many pages of unclear legal speak. Many promises were given including United indicating that they have empowered their people to offer as much as ten thousand dollars as an inducement for a passenger to give up their seat. Let's see how that goes, the proof of the pudding is in the eating.

---

[145] (wwwMOXNEWScom 2017; Mindock 2017)

Richard Solomon

The Importance of Empowerment

Why then is this so important to customers? Why can't customers take what they are given? Why can't they follow the rules, policies, systems, and processes? Why must they continuously ask for more – seeming to never be satisfied with the status quo? The customer is no longer king; the customer is a dictator and the best strategy that any business can have is a satisfied customer. Remember too that **signature** Service calls for VIP service to every customer, every time.

Remember Suzy? Suzy is surprised to learn that she can spend as much as 2000 USD of the company's money to satisfy a guest. She is shocked at this level of empowerment, as she has never been entrusted with such resources and authority before. Had Suzy worked at Caribbean or American Airlines, for example, she would have needed a strong heart (for fear of heart failure) because of the sharp contrast in empowerment.

The result of customer satisfaction is repeat business. And the value of repeat customers cannot be overstated; here are some good facts to remember:

1. They spend 33 percent more than new customers per transaction.

2. They are much easier to sell additional products to: you have 60-70 percent chance to sell more services to current customers, but only 5–20 percent chance to sell to new prospects.

3. Happy customers tell 4 to 5 others of their positive experience and word-of-mouth is still the best way to build any business;

Richard Solomon

satisfied repeat customers telling others about your service is GOLD, just ask Zappos and Amazon.[146]

The chance of customers doing repeat business is higher when they are well taken care of by the people on the front line. Let me say this more directly: The success of your company does not rest in the hands of marketing or engineering; when a customer calls or walks in the door, it rest in the hands of the person on the front line! These employees are unfortunately often the least-trained, least-qualified, least-experienced and least-empowered.

Think about this, would an airline take a 737 jetliner and put it in the hands of someone who is not fully trained and able to handle it? Of course not; that would be ludicrous!!! But this is what companies do every day with their customers; they spend loads of money to get them in the door, and then they get treated like crap.

Pilots, engineers, IT people, and many others have to be trained up the wazoo and then retrained in order to do their jobs well. Well, human customers are more important (not to mention complex) than any system or engineering challenge we face. The plain fact is that our customer service people need to be trained, retrained, and empowered to make decisions that are in the best interest of the customer on the spot.

Why Can't It Always be This Easy?

I suspect you have been caught in the madness of end-of-year holiday shopping, running from store to shop, trying to get that gift in just the right color or size. The malls are usually over crowded and the check

---

[146] (LeBoeuf 2000)

Richard Solomon

out lines can be longer than most people can stand. Online shopping has become a typical method for purchase. Statista Inc. reports that a total of $1.895 trillion was spent globally in online retail in 2016.[147] Amazon.com seems to be leading the way with almost 43 percent of the e-commerce sales in the U.S.[148]

A few years ago, before online shopping was so popular, I decided to do all my end-of-year, holiday-season shopping online. No exceptions whatsoever; everyone was going to get a "web gift," like it or not. In a way, I think some companies put more effort into the online experience, thinking about all kinds of permutations and possible scenarios and ensuring that their online systems can respond. But back to the story.

I used all kinds of online tools to help me sort through a mountain of options for different people. Once I began the search, the search engines asked for a list of parameters including: gender, age, interests, price range, and gift category. They essentially help you to funnel your search to a short list of likely options, thus making your final decision much easier.

For one person, I did not need a search engine. A few months before on an American Airlines flight, I had seen what I thought would be ideal item of jewelry for my wife, who **says** "women can never have enough jewelry or fragrances." I went to the website of the seller of the item, but sadly the site would not process my credit card. I set out in search of a suitable alternative and ended up on Amazon.com, as they had a seller with a similar item.

---

[147] (Statista 2017b)
[148] (Molla 2017)

Richard Solomon

Anyone who has shopped on Amazon knows that the process is usually simple and, if you are a return customer with an account, then in a few clicks you can be done.

Being a happy Amazon customer since 2002, I had purchased from there countless times before. In those days, Amazon was not the online retail behemoth it is today, but the basic model was already in place. At the time, Amazon had annual sales of just $3.9B; and 7,800 employees.[149] Compare this with its numbers in 2016: annual revenue of $135.98B; net income of $2.371M, and 341,400 employees. I guess the phrase "you've come a long way baby" is fitting.[150]

Back to My Story

Maui Divers Jewelry is a Hawaiian-based jeweler that manufactures and sells handcrafted pieces. The shiny, diamond-encrusted, slipper pendant was my final choice. Happy with what I saw, I placed the order; simple, easy peasy. Within an hour, I received a call from someone identifying themselves as a CSR from Maui Divers; she was very apologetic and quickly informed me that the item I ordered was actually out of stock. I was naturally disappointed, for which she was prepared.

The adroit service pro simply said: "We are sorry about this mix-up. I have identified a few pieces that are close to the one you originally ordered. Would you be willing to look at these to see if any of them would be a fitting replacement?" Notice that the CSR gave me an option, rather than telling me what I had to do. Adults generally do not like being told what to do. Instructions like "you have to call

---

[149] (Encyclopedia.com 2017)
[150] (Kaplan 2017; Bishop 2017)

Richard Solomon

again" or "take a number and have a seat" are rarely seen as positives by customers.

On examining the options, I settled on one that wasn't much different to the original choice. As it turned out, the replacement was about 25 percent more expensive than the original choice. Once I informed the CSR, she was quick to say: "Very good choice. I would be happy to ship this out to you immediately with no added cost to your original purchase price." I am so sorry that I don't remember her name, but she was deft, quick, and pleasant; she never put me on hold to refer to her supervisor; nor did she try to make me pay the added 25 percent. She was ready to make an empowered decision in the best interest of the customer, full stop!

Why can't it always be this easy? How many times do your customers have to fight with a rule, a CSR, or a policy so that they could be treated with respect, sensibly, or just right? Many companies out there could use a dose of empowerment, allowing their people to just do the right thing in favor of the customer.

What is This Thing Called Empowerment?

Empowerment is giving the employee the latitude to do what is necessary to satisfy your customer — NOW! I know it sounds scary on the surface, to give that kind of power to the frontline. But empowerment is not blanket power or decision-making authority – accountability must be included. Think about it: if your front-line people can't do what is needed to make customers happy, then you might as well stop spending all those precious marketing dollars to get the customers to do business with you in the first place. Why would

Richard Solomon

you work so hard to bring them in while, at the same time, tying the hands of your biggest group of people who ultimately will make your customers happy or want to defect?

The hard truth is: If your people are not willing or able to make decisions that have not been pre-approved by management (for any reason), then they are simply not empowered! When an employee comes up with an idea that is different from what has been tried in the past and they get shot down without reasonable consideration and dialogue, there is no empowerment. When an employee goes outside the lines and does something unconventional to make customers happy, and they get chewed out for it, there is no empowerment. If an employee wants to give away **a little value** to make up for a mess the organization made but has to come to the manager or supervisor to get approval, then there is no empowerment. It's that simple!

You may be thinking that these are extreme positions to take, and you are totally correct, they are extreme. In this extreme market, with extreme competition, and extreme options, extreme empowerment is a strategic advantage.

So Why Is Empowerment So Low?

The BIGGEST answer is FEAR!!! **Many leaders are afraid** that customers will milk the system and employees will be complicit and give away the store. Research has shown that only 3 percent of customers want something for nothing. Most customers are happy to pay for the products and service they receive. Sure, everyone wants a good deal, but wanting something for nothing is just not how most customers are wired. If you doubt this for a minute, think about yourself; when you go to purchase something, do you spend time thinking how you can get it for free, how you can outsmart the organization and score? No, you don't. When you go with buying in mind, you go prepared to pay, so why would other people be any different. Wanting a great deal is very different from wanting something for nothing.

In addition, there is a certain pride attached to paying your way. The majority of people do not aspire to be freeloaders despite what some believe; we have been trained from very early to go to the store and get what we need in exchange for payment. A mistake that many companies make is that they design systems and policies to catch the 3 percent who go against this norm; they fail to realize that these systems and policies also punish the 97 percent who are happy to pay their way. Another point is that, if you have done a decent job hiring right, orienting, training, and building strong systems with accountabilities, you should not really have to worry about people giving away the store.

I recall a family trip that ended unfortunately. On arrival to our destination, we realized that one of our bags never made it. That bag belonged to my daughter and contained, among other things, her new graduation dress – oh dear! We did the usual reporting to the airline but despite what they say were their best efforts and my repeated calls to several airports, no luck and no bag anywhere. We were eventually offered compensation that was oh so low and simply did not cover the bag and its contents. I was told that their compensation policy was based on some ancient rule that airlines had agreed to decades ago. Being the customer that I am, I complained all the way up to the VP of

Richard Solomon

Customer Service, who eventually bent the rules and gave me business class level compensation plus 2000 USD in travel vouchers for my trouble. I considered this compensation not only adequate but also smart. The travel vouchers would keep me as a customer, virtually ensuring that I did not end the relationship with the airline at that time.

I choose not to name the airline or the VP because, as I sat in his office, we talked less about the unfortunate bag loss and more about the obvious prevailing belief within the airline that customers are out to scam them. He was relatively new to the company and had had a long career in aviation by this time. I put on my consultant's hat and asked about their systems and authority levels. With obvious frustration he told me how hard it was to even get sign off on these travel vouchers. **The VP of customer service could not easily get sign off on travel vouchers to appease an unhappy customer!!! Why does he need signoff anyway?** Within months of that experience, he had resigned from airline, I suspect the frustration was too much.

The other **fear is on the part of employees**; many are afraid to step out and do what is in the best interest of the customer if it's not exactly according to the rules and policies. More than likely, they have been chewed out before or have witnessed their colleagues suffer the same fate for some minor deviation. Remember the five monkeys?

The more you think about it, the easier it is to realize how silly this approach is. For example, a telecom that I provide services to had a

Richard Solomon

problem with customer churn[151]. Their customer base grew faster than the inherited network could be upgraded and expanded to meet the ever-increasing demands of customers. Things would slip through cracks sometimes, resulting in customers deciding to terminate their accounts. The people on the front line knew that there were challenges in the system, but the hoops they had to jump through to get approval to spend a little of the company's money to save the customer was just too much. Too many customers left without so much as a slight effort on the part of the company representatives to retain their business.

Water at the Westin Dawn

I was recently hired to conduct some workshops for a client and the sessions were timed to coincide with a regional customer service conference at which I also spoke. Additionally, I conducted a training course on "Aligning Culture to Strategy." Everything was held in Sint Maarten, a Dutch constituency of the Kingdom of the Netherlands located in the Caribbean. The island is also home to French Saint Martin, and there is no physical border, with both residents and tourists moving freely from one side to the other. At the border points, you can literally stand in two countries at the same time (pretty cool).

My multiple engagements required an eight-day stay and the client decided on the Westin Dawn Beach Resort. Generally, all went well: The restaurant staff were particularly good, and the front desk was speedy and responsive. Every room service order delivery was followed by a call to ask how everything was. The rooms were much larger than your typical hotel room, and once I pressed a little, they

---

[151] Churn is the word used to describe the rate of customer defection in some industries.

Richard Solomon

found me a suite directly facing the oversized pool and beach. You could tell that a lot of planning, training, and effort had gone into creating a memorable customer experience.

But as you know by now, I tend to attract the strangest customer service interactions. I had a most curious experience about halfway into my stay. In addition to coffee, tea, and such supplies, every evening someone would come by to refresh bottled water. On one such occasion, I simply asked for a second bottle instead of the usual one. "Sorry but we are out of water" was the reply. I was surprised to say the least. So you are saying that the hotel has no more bottled water, I asked. She quickly responded, "yes, we are all out, I put in an order and I am awaiting delivery." Incredulous! Now you don't have to be a business major to know that the person who delivers bottles of water to guest rooms is most likely not the person who does the ordering, certainly not in a resort with hundreds of staff and 317 rooms. Nor are words such as "order" and "awaiting delivery" usually used to refer to internal processes, these are used to refer to external supplier actions.

She left, but it weighed heavily on my mind: Why would this young employee feel the need to tell such a tall tale. I called the operator and said: I understand there is a shortage of bottled water in the hotel? "No, we have no shortage," the voice on the other end said, but this is what I was told. Now is where it begins to get really interesting. "But I was told that they delivered water to your room..." came the explanation from the operator. As it turns out, the hotel has in a place a one-bottle-per-room policy (undoubtedly to drive sales of the grossly overpriced bottles in the mini bar).

Richard Solomon

My concern was not that they were trying to push overpriced water, not at all. Actually, this might make good business sense if you recognize that your customer has the flexibility and willingness to pay. My issue was why would this person either feel so disempowered or scared about just giving a customer another bottle of water with a cost of 15 cents, that they would opt to come up with such a ridiculous story???!!! My conversation with the operator ended with a sarcastically comment, telling her to please have a case sent up and kindly bill my room (ok yes, I can be extra at times).

The concerned voice of the manager on duty was next on the line; she apologized and told me that while they do have a "one-bottle guideline" (note she did not say policy or rule), staff are free to give more if guests ask. It was either the employee was disempowered or there was something that told her that I should have no more. Within minutes of that exchange ending, the manager was at the door with several cold bottles from the bar and a warm apology. I hope they look into the possible dis-empowerers in that situation.

The Cost of Disempowerment

On a recent business trip to Abuja Nigeria (or mission as one of my colleagues prefers to call it), my client booked me into the most convenient hotel available. Convenient in this case meant that it was literally next-door to the project location. No taxi, no waiting no traffic (driving in Abuja's is quite an interesting experience), just a 1-minute walk and I am there.

Being of West African decent, I always have to resist the polite urgings of the immigration officers to get into the line for citizens. One officer once asked me "are you sure?" when I said I was not a citizen. The trip to the Top Rank Hotel was uneventful; it was when I tried to check in that I realized that there would be efficiency and empowerment challenges here. The polite young man at the check-in desk had no record of my pending arrival, although I had a letter from the hotel signed by the manager confirming my reservation, the rate and a booking number.

He eventually contacted someone by phone that gave him the authorization for the corporate rate (which is typically lower than the rack rate). Let me quickly get to the empowerment part of this story. Suffice it to say that every room we moved to had problems, the infrastructure was just not well maintained and the Wi-Fi access was a total disaster. So much so that my client loaned me a wireless modem so that I could have more reliable connectivity.

The night manager offered to move me to the diplomatic suite because I complained bitterly about a leaking sink that was causing a slipping hazard (it had been supposedly repaired the day before). He insisted that a porter take me to the suite for my approval before I moved again (this would be the 3rd time). The room was practically the same as the previous ones but had fewer problems, so I said yes. This is where the story got interesting; he then called the room to tell me that I had to pay an increased rate. Are you kidding me? Are we in the twilight zone! Why would you even think to ask me to pay more after such a terrible experience and **you giving me the option to move to this room?!**

He went on to explain that the room was in a higher category and he could not give it to me for the same price, I quietly said I would come to speak with him face-to-face. "Not one Naira more!" was my very clear and firm comment to him, if I must pay more to get a half decent room then I would be checking out the next day. He spent the next several minutes on the phone explaining to a superior that I was unhappy and that I had originally booked for 23 nights but was prepared to leave after just 4 due to the condition of the hotel. The senior finally gave his blessing and they *let* me have the room for the lower rate. Now get this, the night manager could not make a five thousand Naira (about fourteen dollars) decision. Situations like these are not comfortable for customers, I witnessed the call and could see his discomfort, which in turn made me uncomfortable.

The thing is that the staff at the hotel were some of the nicest I have every encountered, always smiling, pleasant, helpful and polite. The IT person did his best, he was very apologetic and suggested that I could come to the business center, as the Wi-Fi signal seemed to be strongest there. But the general hotel infrastructure only gave so much. The staff were always willing to help and never seemed burdened by whatever request I made. They were happy to move us to another room or to try to repair whatever issues they could, but in the end we opted to change hotels after 7 nights, it was just too much.

There were two problems here, one was the infrastructure itself, it was somewhat old, low quality and in need of proper maintenance. But the other was that the staff were not empowered to make even the smallest decision that deviated from the letter of the law. The Sandralia, just a 5 minute walk or a 2 min taxi ride away was super happy to welcome us for the balance of the stay. Not much difference in price, but extremely superior in infrastructure and facilities. Top

Richard Solomon

Rank's lost due to poor facilities and disempowerment was Sandralia's gain.

Barriers to Empowerment

There are a few barriers that stand in the way of employees acting with empowerment. Smart, well-meaning employees are thinking employees, and they want to make smart decisions that will help the customer and grow the business. Now if you hired wrong, oriented wrong, trained wrong (or did not train and orient at all), and managed wrong, do not expect your people to step up and give, do, think anything more than the bare minimum. If you are doing the other parts right and they are not acting with empowerment, check for the following barriers.

Barrier # 1 – No Purpose

People are more inclined to act with power when they understand the bigger reason behind their work. Front-line employees need to believe in something big, and they need to see how their effort at serving the customer connects with an overarching purpose. FedEx is in the courier or package-delivery business, but when that package is a gift for a special occasion, a piece of equipment which, if not delivered on time, could cripple the company, or an organ for life-saving surgery, you can see how the status of what FedEx employees do changes. In the words of founder and Chairman Fred Smith, "we transport the most important cargo in the world."

Here are some things you can do to add purpose to the work of your people:

Richard Solomon

1. **Promote the purpose:** Talk about the **signature** service vision. Let people know what you see for the organization and how what they do impacts the customer and their lives.

2. **Give people context to their work:** Don't just give expectations; tell the what, why, when, and who. Think of it this way: If you are painting a picture of a man in a boat fishing, you will include the water, the trees, rocks, sky, and other elements that give the main subject context and the painting meaning. Do the same with your people.

3. **Cheer on the heroes and sheroes:** Humans learn well from stories. When you find examples (go looking for them) of empowered service, ensure that they are told throughout the organization. It's not enough to just make someone employee of the month. When there is a service or empowerment connection, tell their victory stories to everyone with pride.

4. **Live the purpose:** If service is the most important focus of your business, it should be **your** most important focus too. Be sure that your everyday actions with customers (internal and external) reflect the same purpose you preach.

Barrier # 2 - No Protection

Fear can be defined as the anticipation of future pain or discomfort; employees often worry that there will be no cushion to ease their fall in case they mess up. This anticipation of future pain is enough to prevent even the most well-intended employee from coloring outside the lines.

Richard Solomon

Don't get me wrong, offering protection does not mean a lack of accountability. Holding others accountable for their actions and choices is necessary, but this is not the same as making it a tightrope act for employees to think for themselves. We need policies, rules, systems, and procedures, but it's just impossible to plan for every situation. So, for service to be **signature**, the employee will have to make some decisions on the front line. You must remove the risk for well-meaning, thoughtful employees. If they mess up (as some surely will), your approach should be one of curiosity and respect, with a desire to understand and help in development. Remember, employees are not insane; their decisions have reasons. Guide them, teach them, coach them, but above all else, trust them.

Here are some things you can do to add protection to the work of your people:

1. **Check your procedures:** Staff may feel hung-out-to-dry because of the way things were handled in the past. Speed and zeal to punish deviations may actually result in the wrong precedents being set.

2. **Check the history:** What happened the last time someone made a mistake or a "bad decision?" Did they get beaten up or chewed out, or was it taken as an opportunity to coach, teach, and grow? If you want **signature** service, you must be prepared to forgive mistakes.

3. **Give employees the benefit of the doubt in public:** Are they inclined to believe that they will be held liable no matter their reason for making an empowered – albeit out-of-the

ordinary — decision? What is the organizational dialogue regarding this? Give them the benefit of the doubt publicly.

4. **Check your own response:** When employees seek support from above them in difficult times, how are they viewed, what is the response? Don't hide or shield yourself from difficulty; when needed, step up and support your people with advice, backup, or authorization.

Barrier # 3 - No Permission

Managers and supervisors (like parents) say 'no' way too often. Even if you have not told your people that they cannot do this or that, if you do not give them explicit permission to act outside the box, they won't. The repeated denial of permission (even in other areas) makes people wary of deviating from the norm. What if they do and you disagree? Will there be a cost? Who will pay? Will they be reprimanded or even fired? Employees need to know openly and explicitly from management that they can think and make sensible decisions, even if they deviate from the norm.

Here are some things you can do to give permission to your people:

1. See employees as smart and reasonable. In so doing, you set yourself up to value their sense of the customer's situation and their input.

2. Seek their counsel from time to time, this lets them know that you value their opinion and input.

Richard Solomon

3. Set the example yourself by modeling responsible flexibility and freedom. Show that you too are prepared to take reasonable and well-thought-out risks that favor the customer.

4. Be sure that those who are creative and take some risks to fix a broken customer relationship are openly praised and rewarded. You may have to examine and change your reward policy, but at the least you can lavish them with praise.

5. Check your rulebook. Is it filled with reams and lists of "you can't" and "don't?" I suspect you could strip away some of the annoying, unhelpful rules that only serve to prevent your people from being flexible with the customer.

Barrier # 4 – No Proficiency

Good old-fashioned know-how is still crucial. People simply need to be proficient at their jobs, and there is no work-around for this. In fact, empowerment is built on a foundation of knowledge. Employees must understand their jobs, the rules, the processes, the systems, and above all else, the **signature** service vision. You may need to train and retrain and demonstrate again and again; some people may need refreshers, do whatever is needed to ensure high proficiency.[152]

It is as one jazz musician puts it: *"The reason that jazz musicians are so good is that they first learn the rules very well, then begin to improvise and break the rules so beautifully that it creates disorderly-harmony which is different and beautiful."*

Here are some things you can do to improve the proficiency of your people:

---

[152] (Bell and Zemke 2013)

Richard Solomon

1. Ensure that everyone is well-trained in the systems and processes.
2. Make sure they understand **why** rules and policies exist and the impact (not necessarily consequences) of bending or breaking them.
3. Recognize and reward those who demonstrate empowerment by using their proficiency and efficiency.
4. Model efficiency and proficiency yourself.
5. Be a lifelong learner yourself.
6. Tell the stories of employees who use proficiency-based empowerment.
7. Push decision making authority as close to the front line as possible.

What to do

1. Trust your people to do the right think.
2. Give your people standard operating practices but don't straight-jacket them.
3. Allow your people to think outside the box and color outside the lines to make the customer happy.
4. Staff must be held accountable for their decisions.
5. Coach and train employees who may need help in making better decisions.
6. Back-up your people when they take customer-friendly, yet risky decisions.
7. Ensure your people know the purpose, have the protection, proficiency and the permission to act with empowerment.

Richard Solomon

Summary

Let me be clear, my intent here is not for organizations to go off the rails and become unstructured; far from it. In fact, order and structure are what define the whole concept of organizations; after all, they do have to be *organized*. Luckily for us, the majority of customers will be fine with the offerings, systems, and processes as they are presented. If the organization is strong, then you will find that a great many customers will require nothing more than the standard offerings. The trick here is to make "the standard" offerings VIP-worthy. Remember it's about quality.

It is when the requests are different, when the systems don't work, when standard just won't do, that the BIG E (for empowerment) is required. Stories like the one below show the amazing things that can happen when people are empowered.

"Zaz Lamarr's mother had been stricken with cancer, and Zaz thought a pair of shoes might brighten her mom's spirits. However, given the weight loss that can happen with cancer patients, Zaz wasn't sure what size would fit. So, she placed an order with Zappos for several pairs of shoes in a variety of sizes, hoping at least one of them would work. Fortunately, two of the pairs fit and Zaz made arrangements to return the remaining shoes. However, before Zaz could get to the UPS store, her mother took a sudden turn for the worse and passed away. When the Zappos customer service representative (CSR) contacted Zaz and found out why she didn't have time to return the shoes, rather than insisting that Zaz make time to go to the UPS store, the people at Zappos sent UPS to Zaz, and then the

Richard Solomon

next day sent Zaz a beautiful bouquet of flowers to let her know they were thinking of her in her time of need.[153]"

Remember *"70 percent of complaining customers will do business with you again if you resolve the complaint in their favor. If you resolve it on the spot, the number jumps to 95 percent.[154]* Why not take advantage of this by giving your people the power to resolve most problems on the spot? It will increase your repeat business and reduce clutter in the complaint systems, not to mention reduce stress among the front-line workers and management.

---

[153] (R. Collins 2015)
[154] (LeBoeuf 2000)

Richard Solomon

Chapter 9

Map, Manage & Measure the Customer Experience (M3 CX)

In this chapter, we will cover the critical areas of the customer experience (CX) that your company must manage and measure to become a super CRM machine and deliver **signature** service. I will also clearly point out the steps to take to have success in this area. If you or your organization is trying to get your hands around what the customer experience should be like or what to measure, then you absolutely must carefully study this chapter so you know exactly what you need to do.

What About Customer Satisfaction?

Are you satisfied? Was it good enough? Did what was provided meet your needs? These questions seem to point to a state of sufficiency, being provided with just enough to meet the need that exists. Well let's think about it: is what we want to do simply to satisfy the customer? Is that enough to keep them coming back and telling their friends? Is it enough to blow the competition out of the water? Is it enough to keep you at the head of the class? You know the answers to this. Satisfaction is good, but good is simply not good enough in a

Richard Solomon

market of endless rivals, unending demand for more and better, plus a long list of strong substitutes.

Defining the Customer Experience

"What gets measured gets done" is often a true statement, but it assumes that the measurement will result in some reinforcement, improvement, or other action. Companies need to be willing and able to connect the dots from data to value-added action. Measurement and keeping score is non-negotiable if we are to ensure **signature** service for our customers, and superior performance for each other, our investors, and other stakeholder groups. This is a no-fail mission.

Defining the customer experience is not mainly about product research, although you can and should dovetail information from your service measurements into product research and development efforts. Yet, I want to make a clear distinction between product research (with customers) and measuring the quality of the customers' experience you deliver. Purposefully, I have waited until now to introduce the concept of **customer experience management** as it fits perfectly in this chapter on measurement.

We will use the following definition of the **customer experience**: *The customer experience can be defined as the sum quality of the relationship a customer has with a brand over the lifetime of that relationship including all interactions before, during, and after the sale.* The above definition creates a platform from which we can jump into a proper study of the measurement effort. If you truly want to provide **signature** service, you have to get clear on what the customer should experience, what they value, and how to measure your efforts, success, and failures or opportunities.

Customer Service Versus Customer Experience

Let's tackle this business of differentiating customer service from the customer experience. I surprised my wife with a one-week trip to Ft. Lauderdale; it was a busy time of year, but you only have a 25th wedding anniversary once. I rented a luxury one-bedroom suite on the 12th floor overlooking the water. It's a great view right close to the drawbridge on Sunrise, with yachts and other watercraft going by from time to time, and a five-minute walk puts you right on the never-ending Ft. Lauderdale beach.

While at Sawgrass Mills, a shopping center in the area, Shelly made the spontaneous decision to get a manicure/pedicure and I thought I might as well do the same. After all, I would have to wait anyway, plus malls are not exactly my idea of fun. The service at the shop was reasonable enough, although a bit rushed. You could tell they needed to keep people moving through the chairs. They smiled and spoke with fake interest purely designed to encourage you to buy the various upsells. From initial inquiry to paying the final bill along with an undeserved tip, we were in and out in an hour at the most. Not a bad experience, but certainly not a great one; they provided the expected "customer service" that I have sadly come to expect from most organizations.

Approaches to tipping vary the world over, with some organizations expressly refusing customers' efforts to provide a little extra payment to the person who provided the service; while others actively encourage and sometimes downright demand it. Personally, if the service is poor, I sometimes won't tip or maybe grudgingly leave the bare minimum on the table.

In contrast, a few months later we visited the same area and this time picked out a spa after some online searching and reading a few reviews. We eventually opted for a family-owned spa at a new yet small mall; no appointment was needed so off we went. Once we got to the establishment, there was a warm welcome that sounded and felt more like "welcome back." The ceilings were high; there was soft relaxing music and soft chairs. As soon as Shelly went into the actual spa section, I sat down to wait and, as usual, broke out the laptop to use my time productively (no, I am not a workaholic – that's my story and I am sticking to it).

The young lady who welcomed us quickly told me that there was a waiting room just across the hall. I walked across the corridor and sat in the soft reclining chair. She soon appeared with a bottle of water and, without being asked, offered me the Wi-Fi password. Twenty minutes passed and again she came to see how I was doing (remember I was not the actual customer), asking if I wanted to go check on my wife. She showed me the way and smiled as I returned to the waiting room. When the process was completed, I paid the bill along with the well-deserved tip and left to a cheery farewell. Shelly had a very similar experience with her attendant. It sounded like she had met an old friend by the way she spoke about their interaction. From entrance to exit, we felt like VIPs, as if the entire place, system, process, and people were designed just to take care of us (in fact it was).

Richard Solomon

To make this explicit, here are a few contrasting facets of customer service and customer experience:

Reactive vs. Proactive

Customer service is intended to meet an obvious or overt need that is expressed by the customer. You take your car in for a service; the CSR checks in your vehicle, gives you a couple documents to sign, and tells you that they will call you as soon as it's ready. Wouldn't you prefer that, as you bring in the car and it gets checked in, they have a loaner waiting for you and the CSR tells you that they will call you with an update in 3 hours? Or even better, give you the option of waiting in a comfortable room as the service will only take 2 hours?

Transactional vs. Relational

The language and the process of most customer service interactions are pretty scripted and clinical. "Good day, welcome to the Crusty Crab, may I take your order?" A reasonable greeting, but wouldn't you prefer: "Hi my name is Kelly, welcome to the Crusty Crab, we just took some mini patties off the grill, would you like to sample one while you decide on what you want to order?" If you replied that you weren't interested in the sample, the response would be something like: "no problem, but I might just have one myself; they are really that good!" Who could resist at least a smile to such a witty greeting?

Efficient vs. Effective

We generally think of efficiency as being with things, processes, and systems; it focuses on maximum productivity. Effectiveness takes in a wider swath that includes efficiency, but also focuses on *how* that efficiency is achieved. Think of checking into a hotel where you have stayed before; efficient would be a speedy check-in, reservation easily found, dates and rates correct, keycard in hand and off you go. Effective would be all those things, but could also include: "how was your trip?" or "which airline did you fly in on?" or even "are you hungry? I could call the kitchen and have something whipped up for you."

Customer vs. VIP

We are all unique, each with our own quirks, foibles, and idiosyncrasies. Yet we all have similar desires: to be healthy, secure and happy. We all make a living through some type of work and no matter where on the economic ladder we are, we want to get value for our money. When we purchase a product or service, there is no doubt that we feel a great need to be treated with respect and fairness.

General customer service interactions tend to be less helpful and careful, while VIPs usually get more help and care than most fully functional adult humans actually need. Here is an example: if you visit a coffee shop, you fully expect to line up as you wait your turn to get to the cashier. Once there, you are expected to know what you would like, place the order, pay and stand to the side as the barista prepares your drink, or find

Richard Solomon

a table and maybe scan the online news for a few minutes. I guess this can be described as the fast-food version of coffee, none-eventful, fairly quick, and hopefully efficient.

Contrast the example above with my experience in a coffee shop a few years ago with my daughters. I had never been there before, and we approached the counter and were smilingly greeted with an invitation to have a seat. They brought the menu and helped us choose the most ideal selections. Shortly after, the waitress brought the order and suggested a snack that would nicely accompany our beverage orders (which we declined). The bill eventually came when it was obvious that we were finished. The cost was not much more than what we would have paid at a more traditional coffee shop. We were seen to the door (which was held open) and bid a cheery farewell.

As a customer, you are treated as one of many to the standard offering, nothing special, nothing unusual. As a VIP, you are catered to, you are an individual with specific needs, and the people, processes, and systems are all in place for *you*. Even though there are others getting the same treatment, it feels like all of this was designed just for you. VIP service is very quick, amazingly efficient, extremely convenient, highly personalized, and relatable.

Can a company provide this level of service to all its customers? Surely the cost would be astronomical? With Information Communication Technology (ICT) being such a service-delivery enabler, companies are able to do more with less by employing this very long ICT lever. They can enhance the individuality of the service without breaking the budget. Think of what Amazon.com has done with their overall service and the added value of Amazon Prime. I am hard-pressed to identify an area where this lever will not apply. Even in our own training and consulting business, we use ICT in just about every area.

Also, it is instructive to remember that as much as 85 percent of customers are willing to pay more to ensure superior service.[155] Simply put, you can charge more when you deliver a **signature** service experience. Table 5 below captures this contrast.

---

[155] (Wolfe 2012)

Richard Solomon

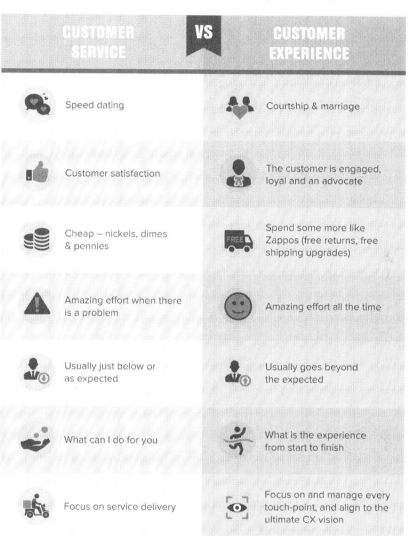

Table 5

Richard Solomon

Designing the Customer Experience

Begin with the end in mind. In Chapter 4, we looked at the importance of having a customer vision and explored a few very good examples. Let's build on the lessons from that chapter to develop this area of designing an ideal customer experience. *...the sum quality of the relationship a customer has with your brand over the lifetime of that relationship, including all interactions before, during, and after the sale.*

Ask the Right Questions

In order to design the ultimate customer experience, we must answer the right questions, and here are a few to get you started:

a. *"How do we want our customers to feel as a result of interacting with our brand?*
   - *Valued, proud, safe, loved, connected, happy, at ease, etc.*

b. *"What adjectives do we want our customers to consistently use to describe our brand?"*
   - *Strong, wise, fun, quick, easy, honest, stable, high quality, etc.*

c. *"What are the* **signature** *components that we must build in to convey those feelings?"*

d. *"How do we make certain that these feelings are conveyed at all stages of the customer experience?"*

Richard Solomon

Map the Customer Lifecycle

What does — or should — your ideal customer lifecycle look like? Plot the steps or stages you want your customer to journey through, what would be most mutually beneficial? Then you can decide how best to optimize each stage. Most experts agree on the following five stages:

I. **Reach**: Getting the attention of the prospect you want to become a customer.

II. **Acquire**: Attracting and bringing the reached prospect into the realm of the organization's influence.

III. **Convert**: Helping the prospect make a decision to buy.

IV. **Retain:** Keeping the customers interested and seeking to sell more to them (cross-selling, up-selling).

V. **Inspire**: Motivating the customer to become a loyal partner and, more desirably, a "brand advocate."

Richard Solomon

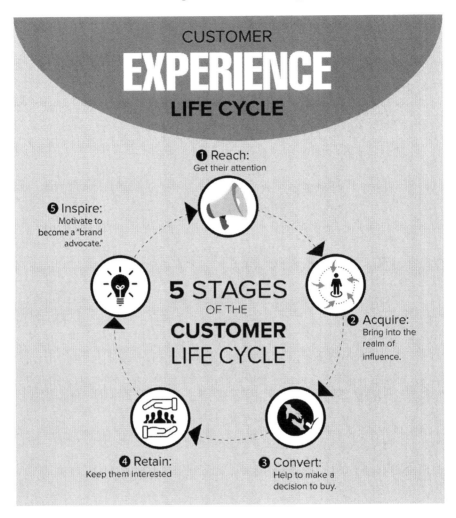

Infographic 35

Map the Touch-points

A touch-point is any way a customer can experience your brand. Touch-points occur at all stages of the customer lifecycle, and few companies have done a better job with them than Apple. Just look at the effort that goes into each stage of the cycle:

Richard Solomon

a. Promotion and advertising that is tasteful, relatable and conveys high quality.

b. Uncluttered website that is easy to navigate.

c. Simple-to-use online shopping with built in up-sells and cross-sells.

d. A clean store layout that is uncluttered and easy to navigate.

e. Many demo units to try.

f. Knowledgeable store associates and genius bar.

g. Quick and uncomplicated check-out process.

h. Packaging that exudes quality and high-end design.

i. Easy set-up with help if you need or want it.

j. Free operating software upgrades for most devices.

Digital Alignment

Digital commerce or e-commerce (too late now but maybe it should have been called d-commerce) as it is called has penetrated deeper into many customer-facing systems. Given that smartphones, smart TVs and smart cars are an integral part of everyday life, it is only natural that customers seek out digital processes to accomplish previously human-driven tasks. 53 percent of millennials[156] would rather lose their sense of smell than their connectivity[157], so obsessed are we with all

---

[156] Persons reaching young adulthood early in the 21st century
[157] (Gayomali 2011)

Richard Solomon

things digital. Added to this, our love affair with smartphones has never been so strong, with penetration rates sitting around 70 percent in much of Europe and North America[158]. It only makes sense, therefore, to build robust digital service delivery and execution systems.

Align the People

Digital processes cannot always accomplish what the customer wants; when this mode falls short or fails, we need humans. Plus, there are some products that simply need a human interface (at least for now). The people must be aligned by first being hired right, then trained and treated like customers themselves.

Sensational Seams

Much has been made in the recent past about seamless experiences in terms of how customers transition between channels, or from one stage of the customer lifecycle to another. In actuality, these seams could be made into sensational events; they are opportunities for you to do something special – something beautiful that impacts the customer in a way that makes an indelible mark on them. Imagine you decided to upgrade your credit card service, maybe after a big promotion or raise, and you have done a great job at managing your balances and payments. As soon as you complete the online application process and hit the submit button, your cell phone rings, it's a live person on the other

---

[158] (Poushter 2016)

Richard Solomon

end thanking you for your ongoing business and the faith you are showing in the company by seeking to upgrade. They tell you that they will personally call within 24 hours once the final approval is made, and discuss some great free extras that you can benefit from. Talk about a sensational seam!!!

Back in the days when timeshares were all the rage, we attended one of those presentations designed to show all the wonderful reasons we should buy their product. My wife and I were one of many couples being shown around, we eventually made it to a large room (sales hall) with tables and chairs. After a fairly short while, I noticed a bell would ring and all the sales persons would clap and cheer; this was to signal that a new owner had just signed up. The celebration would be followed by a bottle of champagne popping open. This is an example of a sensational seam.

Managing all Touch Points

Leave nothing to chance, don't fall into the trap of assuming that you have hired "good people," and everything will fall into place. Nope! Just like the conductor of an orchestra does not assume that his or her symphonic level musicians will all come together well and produce an excellent performance, so too you must not assume. Manage everything, pay attention to every detail; set standards for everything you can, double and triple check process outcomes. Walk backwards and forwards through your systems and test them, critique them and don't be satisfied with good enough.

Richard Solomon

In Chapter 5 we talked about the 3P's of **signature** service (product, processes and people) and pointed to these as the main sources of service challenges. When it comes to managing the customer experience, you have to be obsessive about processes. And even though we cannot create a process or policy for everything, once you realize that there is a need or demand then don't leave it to chance. Yes you have hired right, trained and oriented your people but give them a better chance at success by designing sound and efficient processes. If you realize there is a particular need or a gap, fill it or even empower your people to come up with a process to fill it.

Each stage of the customer life cycle should be linked to a process that is designed to produce an experience in line with your design. For example, let's say a car rental company desires to give customers a smooth, stress-free pick-up experience. Given that most customers reserve cars prior to arrival, and it is fairly easy to get driver's license information at the point of booking; they may simply send clear information (QR or barcode) that gives renters access to the category of car rented. No need to go to the counter, a sign might display names and row numbers, simply choose anyone you like and drive to the exit. Of course this is only an example and may not work in all markets but it would certainly is great when available. No one wants to wait in line to be processed after a flight; people just want to get on their way.

Measuring the Right Things

Once you are clear on the CX vision, the cycle and all touch-points, someone or some group needs to be tasked with making sure that the organization proactively and relentlessly collects feedback from customers at each touch-point and makes meaning of it. If you really believe in this, then go to the full extent and create a position like a Customer Experience Analyst, or take it a step further and set up a Customer Experience Department and don't make the mistake of burying that department within an admin or some shared services division. Go all out and put your money where your mouth is to create a real department with the resources and power to make significant change, headed by a Vice President, Chief Customer Officer or Chief Customer Experience Office who reports into the CEO. Yep, it's that serious, so go hard or go home!

What to Do

In short, if you want your customer to experience the amazingness of your service you must:

a. Measure what your customers are truly experiencing – from their perspective. Go back to chapter 5 for useful guidance on customer feedback systems and listening to the voice of your customer. If you need more help here in terms of developing a customer feedback system, go to *www.thesignatureservicestrategy.com.*

b. Ensure that none of the business metrics sacrifice customer values.

c. Define and map the customer experience and all touch-points.

d. Be proactive rather than reactive.

e. Focus on the relationship.

f. Design everything to give all customers the VIP experience.

g. Align all systems and people.

h. Don't compromise.

Summary

Providing a **signature** customer experience does not happen accidentally; in fact, it requires a very purposeful, focused, and coordinated effort. Think of it as a well-planned and performed symphony, where the experience is wonderful, flawless, heavenly even, but the preparation required is so painstaking that every detail, every component, every element is worked out to the most minute detail.

Your **signature** customer experience can be as beautiful as a symphony. The question is: are you willing to do the work in advance?

Chapter 10

Craft the Right Culture

"When the drummers change their beat, the dancers must also change their steps."

African Proverb

About Culture Crafters and Change Leaders

The people who champion change within organizations and craft cultures come from all disciplines and possess varied skill sets. I have met change leaders who were engineers, accountants and, of course, HR and Organization Development (OD) types. Some of the best change leaders I have met and worked with were not schooled in human capital management or organizational psychology. Although these disciplines help, my experience tells me that there is set of competencies that typify the best change leaders but are not necessarily specific to these disciplines.

1. **Honest Desire for Change**

   This is not so much a competency as it is a state of mind — the honest desire to see your organization transcend its best performance and do even better – to develop a **signature** culture. They have the heart and passion to start, and the commitment to keep going.

2. Know the Business

Once you are part of the organization (as distinct from an outsider), you need to understand how your business works from your specific discipline's point of view, but also from a holistic perspective; you need to have the whole view. It really helps when you have such a vantage point, for it aids in seeing important connections and implications, plus you can speak the language of the organization. Knowing the business also means having the ability to see the business results (both short- and long-term) and the impacts and implications of proposed strategies, tactics and actions.

3. Possess Referent Power

Possibly a leader's greatest source of power, this comes from being respected, admired, and possibly even liked by others. Leaders who are trustworthy, fair, respectful, courageous, competent, and considerate tend to have referent power. They are usually the most honest, empathetic, emotionally intelligent, balanced, and authentic among leaders.

4. Think Strategically

Strategic thinking is analytical and connected thinking. It is both inductive and deductive. The best strategic thinkers can do what I like to call 360-degree thinking. That is being able to consider an issue from all perspectives before deciding on a course of action.

5. The Art of the Long View

Successful leaders of change take the long view; they are able to envisage as-yet unrealized outcomes and have the patience and tenacity to stick with the process for the future payout.

Richard Solomon

6. Understand Leading Change

Finally, good leaders of change understand both the individual and organizational change processes, and instinctively know that change is done *with* people rather than *to* them. They know too that resistance is normal at all systemic levels and it does not scare them. If they don't know these things starting out, they are willing and able to learn them quickly.

If you are looking at the list above and thinking that you don't possess all those qualities, don't worry; the same is true for most change leaders starting out. Most leaders I have worked with did not have all the competencies to begin with, but just as the change effort grows in time, so too does the leader. Don't wait to have all your ducks in a row; start where you are, for you are perfect enough!

A Look at Culture

Have you ever come across an organization that willingly admits that it gives really poor service? I vaguely remember a Papa John's ad some years ago that admitted that they were not as good as they should be. But that is the exception, in fact, most organizations do exactly the opposite; the vision statement, tagline, values and ads all trumpet to the high heavens that their service is the best thing since sliced bread. Naturally, if we are coming up with a vision statement, values, tagline or ads supposedly to lure customers, we won't tell them that the organization is a bungling mess. After all, who airs their dirty laundry in public? However, despite what organizations say about themselves and what they desire to be, who and what they are at their very core is often quite different and shows through the façade they try to create. The true culture of an organization is not necessarily

Richard Solomon

found in the written words, but more so in the daily behavior, attitudes, and actions of its members.

The topic of culture is introduced here **firstly** because if you have gotten this far in the reading, you are likely quite serious about **signature** service. **Secondly**, it is useful to have thought through many of the foregoing elements of the **signature** service strategy before taking the big culture bite. **Thirdly**, in my experience, you can work on all the other factors, but if there isn't a sustained and coordinated effort to adjust the very base fibers of the organization (culture), it is quite probable that there will be a backsliding to the old ways in a short time. According to Edgar Schein, *"organization learning, development and planned change cannot be understood without considering culture as the primary source of resistance to change."*[159]

Once you seek to adjust the status quo, to move the group or organization from the current state to some future state, pushback is natural and to be expected. After all, the way things are has "worked" to this point, and people have been rewarded intrinsically and extrinsically for the habits they have developed.

So, What Is Culture?

The beautiful words and statements written to describe the ethos of the organization do not always reflect its *true* culture. While we spend lots of time and money crafting strategies and oft-include the customer perspective in these, according to Peter Drucker and President of Ford Motor Corp. Mark Fields: "culture eats strategy for

---

[159] (Schein 1992)

lunch!"[160] Remember that, regardless of how amazing our strategies are, they are useless without execution or action. And execution is done by people, and people work within the context of, and are impacted by, organizational culture. I have seen many organizations suffer from a disease I call SPOTS – Strategic Plans on The Shelves. This is where grand plans to change some major part or even all of the organization are stymied by the inability to execute the needed actions.

So, what is this thing called culture and why is it so important for providing **Signature** service consistently? Well I thought you would never ask (ok, I know I asked, but I am hoping you were asking too). I am not a big fan of long-texbooky definitions, but I think this one is useful here: *Organization culture is comprised of a set of values, beliefs, assumptions, myths, legends, and norms shared by members of an organization. It is the invisible yet powerful force that largely defines how its people work, interact, think, decide, and behave.*

Cultural Archetypes

The word 'archetype' is used in a variety of ways and situations, however relying on Jungian[161] psychology helps us understand its use in relation to organization culture; *"a collectively inherited unconscious idea, pattern of thought, image..."* If we incorporate our previous definition with this Jungian perspective, we can conclude that *"an organization's culture is the collectively inherited, often unconscious set of values, beliefs, assumptions, myths, norms and*

---

[160] (Cave 2017)
[161] Carl Gustav Jung – Swiss psychiatrist and psychoanalyst

Richard Solomon

legends that define how its people work, interact, think, decide and behave."

The archetype is a potent concept in the understanding of how culture works. Let's do a little thought experiment. How many wheels does a car have? Most likely you answered four. How many legs does a chair have? Your likely answer is four as well. In both cases you are correct, but are there cars with fewer or more than three wheels? Of course there are, think of a rickshaw in India, a Polaris Slingshot or a "Tuk Tuk" in Mozambique. And three-legged chairs can be found all over the world, as well as "no-legged chairs" including rocking chairs. But why don't our brains easily and naturally go to these other possibilities? Well, it's because we hold an archetype for what a car or chair "should look like" and how it should operate. If other designs are pointed out, we can easily see them as being similar, but they initially escape our minds because the archetype is so well defined, accepted, and ingrained.

Some organizations are known for their specific archetypes and thus *behave* in particular ways. The table (6) below details some examples[162]:

---

[162] (Corlett and Pearson 2003)

Richard Solomon

ORGANIZATION ARCHETYPES

Organization	Archetype	Major Traits
Apple	Outlaw	Break the rules Driven to destroy what isn't working, revolution
Disney	Magician	Transforms what is into a higher-level vision /realize dreams
Jeep	Explorer	Experience freedom; new things Restless yearning to explore the world
Nike	Hero	Exerts mastery, courage, and strength
Oprah Winfrey	Sage	Seeks to distinguish truth and achieve wisdom Understand the world

Table 6

These examples are self-evident, the brands are widely known, and most likely you can easily identify the archetypes from your knowledge of the names presented. These organizations have been able to align their deep archetypal selves to their public faces.

Like organization archetypes, cultures are generally unconsciously held, but are no less powerful. On the contrary, it is possibly *because* they are so invisible and unconscious that they are as potent as they are. The ethos of the organization, its archetypal self, supersedes other factors deemed important, like rules and policies. Despite what an organization may document about itself or what it aspires to, its true

Richard Solomon

self resides deep within. Not seen or touched, this invisible hand wields a powerful force that shapes the employees' behavior and ultimately the customer experience.

Culture is often referred to with statements that lack specificity; regularly these references are to the manifestations of culture instead of the culture itself. It is then useful to examine the three levels of organizational culture. Infographic 36 that follows gives a diagrammatic view of these levels.

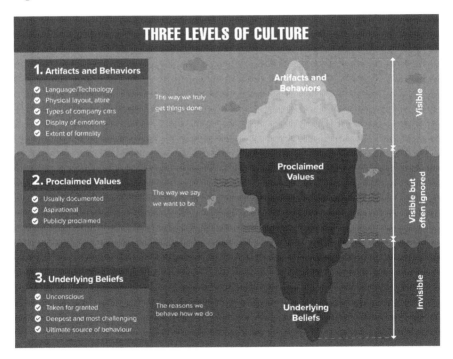

Infographic 36

Artifacts and Behaviors

One way to think of artifacts and behaviors is **what we can see;** these are easily visible to the eye and are usually what people can point to as *the* culture. If a stranger were to visit the organization, the things they would be able to describe include physical layout, dress code, extent of formality, logos, types of company cars, use of names, language, degree of openness, display of emotions, etc. This level is most visible, and manifests itself outwardly but is not always easy to interpret. Artifacts and behaviors actually are not the culture; instead they are the manifestation of it. They show the *what* but do not tell the *why*.

Proclaimed Values

This is the written element, the documented company values and philosophy. If we were to ask company leaders to speak about the organization in a public forum, more than likely we would hear about these values; this is **what they say**. They *should* underlie and determine behavior, but organizations often have two sets of values — the written or proclaimed values and the operating or in-practice values. While they could and should ideally be the same, I have found that, in many cases, the operating values are what we truly live by, while the proclaimed is what we aspire to be. The operating values spring from our underlying beliefs.

Underlying Beliefs

Schein describes these as the unconscious and often taken-for-granted beliefs about the organization.[163] Of the three levels, this is the deepest and most challenging to change. They sit at an unconscious level and are ultimately the source of operating values and thereby actions. They are, however, the most difficult to discern, yet they are key in

---

[163] (Schein 1992)

Richard Solomon

understanding why things are the way they are. This is what people truly, deeply believe in and act on; this is the *why*.

If the organization is to win customer loyalty and deliver **signature** service sustainably, then the very base fibers of underlying beliefs must be shifted. Yet the two higher levels often need to be adjusted in a type of reverse engineering process. In other words, adjusting the artifacts, behaviours and values over time also impacts the underlying beliefs.

What Culture Does

Culture to an organization is like fingerprints to an individual; it distinguishes one from the other and conveys a sense of identity for members of the organization. More specifically, here is a list of functions of culture:

1. Helps employees decide how to interact with each other.

2. Forms a common frame of reference for employees.

3. Serves to unite a large group of employees from a variety of backgrounds, ethnicities, beliefs, and attitudes.

4. Provides behavioral guidance to employees.

5. Helps employees understand what is valued and what isn't.

6. Contributes to the brand image or impression that the public has.

Although invisible, the culture of an organization is super-powerful; Robbins calls it *"the social glue that helps hold the organization together by providing standards for what employees should say and do."* [164] Think of Apple, Disney, or Google: These super-sized organizations can be described in very specific ways. Apple is known for its innovation, Disney for its creativity, and Google for its simplicity. The culture of these respective companies must support the creation and perpetuation of these ways of being.

A practical way of thinking about culture is what it supports and what it discourages. Does the culture support teamwork or more of a lone-wolf approach? What about competition? Are people encouraged to win as others lose, or is win-win a way of life? Is innovation encouraged or are people pressed to color within the lines? What about rules: are there policies for every conceivable situation or is empowerment a staple? Remember the story of the five monkeys? New monkeys quickly adopt the behavior of the older ones without even understanding why. The same is true for humans in organizations; over time, people are so affected by the invisible force of culture that, in spite of their other intentions, they fall into step with the rest of the tribe, for better or for worse.

The Role of Culture in Delivering Signature Service

Signature service is not *just* service; it's VIP service to all customers! And the only way an organization delivers that kind of service is to have all resources working optimally, chief among these (resources) are people. The list of implications of culture on service is literally endless; nevertheless, here are some the most powerful ones.

---

[164] (Robbins 2001)

Richard Solomon

Personalization – The degree to which the organization and its people are willing to bend and twist in order to deliver individual (customized) service. Don't worry about being pulled in every direction; my estimate is that 92 percent of customers are quite content with the standard offerings once the quality, efficiency, and effectiveness are high. It is therefore only a small number that will require a significant degree of personalization.

Empowerment – The extent of trust leaders have in their people and the willingness of those people to make decisions that are in the best interest of the customer and the organization over the long term. Some cultures tend to hold power tightly at the top, refusing to give those closest to the customer the power to do what is in their (the customers') best interest (see chapter 8).

Speed – Organizations move to different drumbeats; some are slow while others are really quick. It is almost as if this timing is set by some unseen metronome. In fact, it is the culture that calls the time, that keeps it in place, and allows people and systems to get things done more or less quickly, even rewarding them for it.

Service Recovery – When things go wrong, as they are sure to, organizations respond differently. That which the organization values will dictate how people respond when service failures occur. In some organizations, people are indifferent, others give a half-baked apology and move on, while others will move heaven and earth to fair-fix the problem and make it up to you.

Costs – Remember that culture impacts how we work and interact in the organizational context; it then has implications for many cost related factors including the extent of bureaucracy, speed, waste, rework, and accuracy. Obviously, these can inflate or reduce cost at multiple levels and systemic points.

Product Development – The extent of innovation, appetite for risk-taking, and inclination to creativity all impact what the organization decides to do and commit resources to in terms of product development, both to new ones as well as improvements. Some companies are wide-eyed dreamers, some conservative, and others extra careful and risk-averse.

How Is a Culture Formed?

Throughout this book, I have pointed to service giants like Disney, Apple and Southwest Airlines. But there are much smaller organizations that exemplify **signature** service.

To outline culture formation, I have chosen an organization I have known and personally interacted with many times for over a decade. The tagline of Advance Dental Care Centre (ADCC), headed by Dr. Curtis Sealy, is *"Simply providing gentle dentistry."* Dr. Sealy has been in private practice for 30 years and our family dentists for the last 10. Amazingly, this 7-chair clinic with a staff count of 30 provides an extremely high quality of VIP service during every single interaction.

Knowing this could not be by accident (*because you just don't stumble unto* **signature** *service*), we sat down at his Chaguanas office to talk about how he built such a robust, customer-focused culture. The very location of the practice is an interesting choice. In those days when he was heading the fledgling startup, many entrepreneurs tried to locate their operation in Port-of-Spain (the capital of Trinidad and Tobago). He decided differently, "flight to quality" was the advice from his economist father. Although an economic concept, the theory was that people would go to the place where the best quality is when the other more convenient choices are of a lesser quality.

Not being formally trained in business, he relied on the same spirit of excellence that he used while at the University of Bristol in the UK: "The only true measure of success is 100 percent."

When the practice was still in its early years, the founder established the standards of excellence: Greet and welcome the patient at the door; treat them like royalty; we all work for the customer – they are everyone's boss —and always deliver what we promised.

As a leader, he deeply believes in age-old principles, principles he teaches to his staff:

- Whatever you do – do it as unto God and

- Do unto others as you would have done unto you.

While Dr. Sealy draws his principles from his strongly held Judaic Christian belief, these obviously cut across religions, cultures, and belief systems. His staff is made up of a variety of beliefs including Hindus, Christians, and others.

A Clear Vision

Sealy is clear about his vision, one that he is extremely passionate about even after all these years: "Perfect VIP service." More than just words, you get the distinct impression that you are important from the way you are treated by all staff. None of the flippant, careless attitudes that we tend to see in so many places. From the door to the chair and back out again, staff are focused, careful and attentive.

Getting the Staff on Board

There are standard qualifications for all categories of dental staff. These being equal, Sealy looks for the right attitude, for without this, they don't stand a chance at ADCC. With the standards firmly in place, all staff are trained in *his* brand of dentistry and made to distinctly understand the level of service expected.

The goodly doctor is admittedly obsessive about quality and tirelessly monitors all components of the operation with a variety of systems designed to capture information on the quality of service the patients receive. He is not casual in the least; he treats this as a life-and-death matter. Deviations and slip-ups are dealt with immediately; feedback, coaching, and training never stops. Resistance to the vision is met with an even stronger dose of vision and standards; this is the way it is, no one is given the latitude to go as they please. Now if you are like me, you probably find this to sound somewhat autocratic, dictatorial even; so it is! This is a service world unto itself and no one is allowed to continually mess it up. His message is simple: You either buy into excellence or this is not the place for you.

Is there high turnover? On the contrary, many of the faces have been in the practice for over 15 years, with those with lesser time only so because they have only been hired as the organization grew. Everyone is given the opportunity and room to grow; at the same time, they are held accountable and given the room to fix their mistakes. Accountability and empowerment are carefully blended together in

Richard Solomon

service of the customer experience. Staff are paid well above market rates and rewarded for excellent performance.

Nothing is left to chance; the music in the car park, waiting room, and clinic are chosen to create a welcoming and relaxed environment. There is a deliberate ratio between parking spots and dental chairs; the design of the office and clinic was done to optimize the patient experience and for maximum efficiency. The patient management system is used to ensure that every patient is treated with utmost care. After a major procedure, each patient receives a call the next morning enquiring how their night was and how they feel. This information is fed back to the doctors and, if necessary, remedial actions taken.

My last question was: "What does the organization still struggle with when it comes to service?" Curtis thought for a silent moment and simply replied "nothing." You see the systems are so deeply entrenched and the mass of staff so strongly bought into the vision, standards of practice, and behaviors that new people have little choice but to be immediately immersed in the culture, a 100 percent VIP Service culture. New people are more likely to follow this overwhelming example than go another way.

Culture Formation: What Dr. Sealy Did Right

Despite not being formally trained in business or organization development, Dr. Sealy instinctively understands several key culture-building components. Let's examine how he formed the culture at ADCC.

Firstly, and possibly most notably, are the greatest power sources of culture formation and that is the **vision, ideology, and early**

actions of the founder(s). Also, founders must model the behaviors they want from their followers. Keep in mind that the way things are now in the organization are significantly due to what has been done before, and the degree of success that the organization has enjoyed with them. The ultimate source of organization culture is its founders and other most-senior leaders and Dr. Sealy set the vision, established the ideology and modeled the expected level of service from the get go.

Secondly, the greatest care is taken in the **selection and training** of staff. You need the right support. Culturally, leaders tend to only hire and keep those employees who think and feel the way they do in terms of the vision and how the organization operates. This is extremely important, but particularly in the early days, as it is these right hires and promotes that will be part of the socialization of newer hires as the organization grows. Not only is who gets hired important, even more so is who gets promoted. This has a two-fold impact: 1. As people go up the management ranks, they are able to influence the culture to greater extents, and these new managers (if properly selected) are then able to further the culture and support the cause. 2. Decisions regarding promotions send a powerful signal to the rest of the organization about what behaviors and values are prized by the organization. Hiring and promoting the right people with the right attitude was critical to success.

Thirdly, **set amazingly high standards**. People need something huge to shoot for that is so much bigger than they are. Don't be shy or compromising in setting standards. If what you want is an organization that is customer-obsessed, then make the customer royalty and show that you mean business. Dr. Sealy's "perfect VIP service," is a lofty standard to keep shooting for.

Fourthly, **reward the behaviors you desire and sanction those that you don't**. Train people and support them in service of their vision-aligned growth, but be sure to reward the right behaviors, for turning a blind eye to misaligned behaviors actually rewards those behaviors and encourages them to flourish.

Fifthly, pay attention to the most crucial issues and **allocate resources in the right places**. As far as you can, don't spare expense and investment when deciding on the systems that will make the customer experience more pleasant. Sealy's clinic layout, piped music throughout the facility and patient management software are all on point. Another such investment is the leader's time, since, where he chooses to focus attention sends a powerful message to the rest of the organization about what's truly important.

Sixthly, ensure that new members are **deeply socialized in the culture** as soon as they enter the organization. People are more open to being influenced earliest in their employment. Onboarding and orientation are non-negotiables. Teach the vision, standards, and processes early; add to this the influence of core staff who have already deeply digested the culture and you have a machine that churns out more and more culture-obsessed proponents. Orienting newbies to his own brand of dentistry helps to socialize and envelope them in the culture.

In a market that is becoming increasingly cluttered with more and more dental establishments, I predict that ADCC's focus on service will continue to make them the stand out option. Their competitors may be increasing in number but they will continue to stand head and shoulders above them all.

How People Learn Culture

People come and go, and today's organizations are not static, nor have they ever been. New people soon learn how things are done around here, what is valued, and the general (and specific) way of being. In most organizations, this is an accidental process, maybe a better word is unintentional; whichever word you prefer, it is useful to identify and understand the most potent ways by which employees learn culture. Knowing these is yet another piece in the culture-change puzzle.

Stories

Sit in the cafeteria or lunchroom long enough and you are bound to hear pieces of fascinating history. Narratives of significant events and people, doing things like rule-breaking, amazing feats, and reactions to challenges that ended in some unexpected outcome. These stories are powerful tools to reinforce and teach cultural values throughout the organization, and are especially useful when orienting new employees. Think of the story of Sam Walton insisting that an employee "take back" a product that the customer bought at the store that was there prior to Walmart's arrival (no-hassle returns), or a junior employee chartering a jet for a customer at Southwest — all in the name of service and not getting fired. Stories like these signal to everyone else what the organization truly values.

Heroes and Sheroes

People who stand out positively become famous within the organization, stories are told about them, and rituals oftentimes focus on them. The internal narrative tells of their heroics and great accomplishments. Very often the formal talent and human resource management systems also make positive examples of these heroes, promoting them to more senior positions and further making their actions even more powerful culture purveyors.

In the same manner, there are those who become infamous due to their attitude or actions that may have earned them a certain reputation. Left unchecked, these people become famous for the wrong reasons and may actually send the message that we say one thing and allow another. On the other hand, if checked, the stories send an aligned message about what is expected and accepted.

Rituals and Ceremonies

Organization rituals and ceremonies communicate and reinforce which goals and achievements are most important. These (rituals and ceremonies) are recurring activities enacted on important occasions or triggered by some particular outcome. Examples include the ringing of a bell when a certain type of sale is made; dousing teammates with cold water or champagne after a sporting victory, or medals/trophies given at a ceremony to members who have achieved success.

Material/Cultural Symbols

Like artifacts, these communicate the culture by silent messages. When you go to a business place, you naturally get a sense of its vibe; is it formal, tensed, fun, serious, etc.? This demonstrates how powerfully material symbols communicate the organization's character. Just like how they communicate to you as an outsider, they express to insiders who and what is important, the degree of quality expected by top management, and the behaviors that are appropriate. As an example, a company may have a pin or a T-shirt or cap with a certain logo for a particular level of performance. Certain positions may have offices on certain floors and car size or parking spots location may vary by rank.

Language and Communication

Whole organizations, divisions, departments, and units within have language by which it and its members are identified. By learning and using the language, members signal their acceptance of the culture and that they are subsumed within it; greater still, they also show their inclination to perpetuate the culture. Much of how culture is learned has to do with what employees repeatedly see and hear; repeated exposures to key messages work well.

Managerial Decisions

In many ways, this last culture-learning method can be seen in greater and lesser amounts within all the previous ones. Management has power over resources and they occupy highly visible positions that show what is important. Their decisions in such areas as hiring, promotions, onboarding, empowerment, company policies, and rewards all serve to signal to the body corporate what is expected, and who and what is important.

View of a Culture

Organizational culture is a descriptive term, for it shows how stakeholders perceive elements of the culture and not whether they like them or not. This point of clarification is helpful, as to venture into whether they like the cultural elements or not treads on the

Richard Solomon

domain of job satisfaction when taking employees' view. [165] Often when a culture is examined, we consider how certain important characteristics are perceived (mostly by employees and managers). Examples can include the following:

1. Innovation and risk-taking
2. Quality
3. Productivity and efficiency
4. People focus
5. Aggressiveness
6. Stability

While delving into how descriptors like those above are seen as useful for a total culture view, let us make this discussion more pointed to our subject of **signature** service by solely examining the customer-related elements of an organization's culture. Taking a prompt from Freire's cultural archetypes, we make one major change and that is to examine one archetype versus multiple. [166] We thus focus on the single cultural archetype of customer-centricity and examine organizational elements through *this* lens alone.

We are now looking at organizational culture as it relates to customers, the degree of customer-centricity and elements that impact the customer experience (directly or indirectly). These all contribute to enhancing or reducing the quality of the customer experience over the life of their employment with the organization. Empowerment, speed, quality, innovation, cost, flexibility, and listening to the voice of the customer are all possible inclusions. For

---

[165] (Robbins and Judge 2013)
[166] (Freire 2007)

Richard Solomon

better alignment, completeness and ease of reference, let's examine the elements we have discussed in chapters preceding (you could choose to include others in your own assessment):

1. Clarity of service vision

2. Leaders go first

3. Listening to the voice of the customer

4. Hiring right

5. Focus on ongoing training

6. Empowerment

7. Map, manage and measure the customer experience

8. Employee engagement

To do a robust job at examining a culture, you need to use an instrument that would be best suited to the elements you want to investigate. Often, surveys are used as these allow respondents to give their perspective and then the responses are aggregated or express them in other useful forms. For certain elements, however, a more objective assessment would be in order. Whereas with empowerment for example, we would seek the opinions of people in the organization (possibly by a survey), for ongoing training, we could measure hours spent per year, number of training opportunities per period, type of training, participant reactions, and transference of learning.

Once data has been gathered on each element, my preferred approach is to analyze the data and make meaning of it; in other words, ask: *"What is this saying about our culture?"* Additionally, it is useful to plot the results visually like the **Signature** Culture Perspective Wheel (see infographic 37 below). This gives a simple yet impactful representation of where the organization is in each area, and indicates the weaker areas (closer to the middle), at which point you could decide what plans to build and then actions to take.

Infographic 37

Remember that this list is not exhaustive; you may choose to use all the items here or alter the list in some way. You will note that I chose to include employee engagement in my Signature Culture Perspective Wheel, although it was not included as a specific topic in the preceding chapters. This is so because employee engagement obviously impacts service quality, and while I did not speak to it directly here, it is implicit in many of the other chapters. Choose those elements that will give a true and meaningful picture of your own culture as it relates to **signature** service.

How to Change a Culture

I wish I could start the last section of this chapter by saying that changing an organization's culture is a simple undertaking. Unfortunately, this is not the case; the fact is that culture change is a significant challenge and requires great commitment, focus and effort. The good news is that it is definitely possible and there are many examples of amazing change and transformation to learn from.

We previously discussed the importance and process of leaders going first, setting a clear vision, hiring right, and orientation and training. All of these are part of the culture change process. However, let us put them and some other steps into a workable process.

Best Culture Change Conditions

Before we examine a recommended process for changing an organization's culture, it is useful to note that there are certain conditions under which such change is most possible. Be careful to keep in mind that there are no exactly ideal conditions or perfect circumstances, nor should you remove any possibilities (other useful conditions) from the table.

1. A Major Crisis:

People are more inclined to act when the boat springs a leak, the bigger the leak, the bigger the inclination. When something happens

Richard Solomon

that disrupts the status quo or calls into question the way we are now or our culture, it's time to take a deep inward look. An example of this might be loss of market share or a major account, or a competitor moving leaps and bounds ahead in technology, manufacturing, or falling customer satisfaction scores.

2. Turnover in Leadership:

When new leaders are installed, there is a silent expectation (a hope even) that things will change. Also, new leaders bring a different set of eyes and experiences to a crisis or any situation. This combination sets the stage for change.

3. New, Young and/or Small Organization:

Younger organizations tend to have cultures that are less entrenched. Small companies usually have fewer layers and less people, making it easier to communicate new values and ways of being. Leaders are more accessible and visible in a smaller organization, allowing them more immediate and wider influence on the culture.

4. Weak Culture:

Where a culture is deeply rooted and widely held by members of the organization, there is strong agreement on who and what we are, it is then more difficult to change. Weaker cultures are therefore more susceptible to change than strong ones.[167]

Culture-change Process

There are many examples where an organization did not follow the "best practices" or the documented theory, and my own client work

---

[167] (Robbins 2001)

Richard Solomon

reflects this. One *Fortune* 50 client I have consulted with on a major culture change initiative showed this reality. They favored John Kotter's 8 Step Process for Leading Change, [168] and while it's a tried-and-tested approach, we realized that the level of mistrust for leaders was so very high that we needed to work on that first. In another case, this African telecom's project office was trying to initiate needed changes from their project perspective. Getting the top leader's public support helped a bit, but they were not gaining much traction. What was missing was the involvement of the trade union/labor leaders.

The organization is a living, breathing organism, so keep an open mind that best practice will not always work well in every situation. Do not be afraid to alter a recommended step or experiment with something new in service of the change you seek to create. These steps are based on John Kotter's 8 Steps of Leading Change and presented in the best order I know; there will be cases where you have to change the order. You cannot hope to apply this or any approach in a clinical fashion; instead, seek to implement, review, adjust, and re-implement as needed.

Step 1 – Sense of Urgency: People need a real reason to change, and there has to be some major need or challenge that pushes the organization and people to be different and do things differently. For most organizations, money is being left on the table because the service quality is simply not where it should be. You should not have to look too far. There is a famous article published by *Fortune* magazine in 1993 entitled *"Times are Good? Create a Crisis."* They described how several companies including Pepsi were doing very

---

[168] (Kotter 2012)

Richard Solomon

well, but felt the need to shake things up before it was too late, look around, and find where the organization is slipping or getting beaten.[169] Of course you should naturally go back to chapter 2 on making the business case and identify a significant reason for change.

Step 2 - Leadership Group Championing: You will need a group of senior leaders who have real power to make changes and who believe in the culture-change effort. They must realize that it cannot be business as usual and be prepared to model the new desired behaviors. Often it is necessary to at least have the blessing or sponsorship of the most senior executive or at least from the suite of chiefs.

Step 3 – Vision: If you aim at nothing, you are sure to hit it! Where are you going? All change initiatives need a destination; in this case, what do you want the new culture to look like? Resist the urge to describe what you don't want or what you want to have go away, this tends to cause efforts to decrease as the problem reduces. Take the time to illustrate in detail what you *do* want. Remember this is what people will rally around, and what will keep the effort focused.

Step 4 - Change Army: Leaders are not able to make major sustained change happen on their own. Sometimes called change champions, this is a group that can be about 5-10 percent of the organization that will serve to promote important changes deeper in the company. The intent is to have no more than two degrees of separation between each employee and a member of the change army. Said differently, no person should have to look farther than two steps up, down, or across the organization to find a change soldier.

---

[169] (Dumaine and Furth 1993)

Step 5 – Communicate: Each step of the process needs communication. The effort to change the culture will be led by a powerful group of leaders and supported by a change army, but everyone in the wider organization needs to be impacted by the effort. They need to see and feel that things are happening, and it is not business as usual and that we are winning. This is not a silent effort. For each of these stages, you should answer the following questions:

- What are the objectives of this communication?
- Who needs to know?
- What do they need to know?
- When do they need to know it?
- Who should tell them?
- How should they be told?
- How many times should they be told (repeated exposures are best – as many as 7 times)?
- Do we need feedback?

Essentially, you are building a communication plan to accompany all the steps and actions taken.

Step 6 – Plan for Action: So now on to the good stuff – planning! Yes, I know, we all want to get into action as quickly as possible, but culture change is not just any project, because there are so very many variables with way too much at stake. You are better off thinking things through before going into action.

Earlier in this chapter, we covered two areas that are imperative to planning and action; these are culture formation and learning.

Essentially your plan for action should answer the following questions:

- What do we want the new culture to look like (revisit the vision – step 3)?
- What culture (re)formation actions must we take and in what sequence?
- How will we ensure that employees learn the new values and behaviors, and which learning tools are best to facilitate this?
- What communication is needed (see step 5)?
- What must leaders do to champion this change?
- What must change agents do to support this change?
- What operational adjustments are needed (reward systems, production schedules, performance management, quality standards, etc.)?

Step 7 – Take Action: Action taking or execution is where the rubber meets the road. Taking action has everything to do with executing the plan you developed in step 6. In his book, *The Spirit to Serve*, J.W. Marriott of Marriot International describes this kind of change as similar to flying a 747 and changing the engine mid-flight. You have to keep the organization operating, but the changes must happen simultaneously.[170] Strategies *say* easy, but they *do* hard and when it comes to culture change, they do even harder.

Come in closer and let me share two very important secrets with you that can either make or break your effort; the first is something I like to call **organizational schizophrenia**. This sets in when the

---

[170] (Marriott 1997)

Richard Solomon

status quo is threatened, and the second is the **availability and dedication of resources** to take different action. [171] Now a **word of caution**: Both of these are huge topics in their own right and can easily fill another book completely. But fear not, here are some approaches that I have used with clients to help them overcome these two obstacles; follow them and you will get amazing results.

1. Organizational Schizophrenia

Remember that the organization is a *"living, breathing organism,"* and like any animal it seeks to protect its turf and way of life. It wants predictability and tries to minimize the unknowns – thus reducing risks and threats. This remains true even though it is the said organization that has identified the need to change and is pushing to make that change a reality. In times like these, it is not unusual to see/hear messages like: *We want innovation and risk-taking, but don't make mistakes. Or we need to move faster at execution, but let's complete another round of analysis (the 5th round!!!) before we sign off.* Another famous one I have met is when *leaders proclaim that it is the type of leadership that must change to propel the organization forward, but are the same ones who leave the meeting and go do the exact opposite to what they just proclaimed.*

These incongruent messages are a sure sign of Organizational Schizophrenia; very often the messages come from different angles, levels or sources, and are not always verbal. When you hear the CEO say that *we are all about collaboration,* but the

---

[171] (Kotter 2012)

Richard Solomon

accounting and reward systems are structured to reward individual performers, then you know there is a schizophrenia problem. This is a contradiction and double bind and the new culture won't take hold.

Returning to our central theme of service, my suggestion is like what my mom used to say: "take only what you can eat." Choose one (or two) powerful elements of the **signature** service culture, think them through and plan for all the probabilities you can think of and start there. You are far more likely to be successful this way than trying to eat the whole elephant at once; simply go one bite at a time. Just in case you are thinking that, at this rate, the new culture will take a significant time to be established, you are very right.

Let's say you decide that empowerment is the first culture component you want to develop and imbed. Here are a few questions you need to have solid answers to:

- Where is disempowerment showing up?
- What are the results of disempowered actions?
- What's holding empowerment back now?
- Who needs to be more empowered?
- How do we want people to demonstrate their new empowerment?
- How could this (empowerment) affect our operations? How should/would we respond?
- What will we do when people mess up?
- How will we reinforce the empowerment messages?

Richard Solomon

- How will we make sure that managers and other leaders practically facilitate and support empowerment?

- How will we let others know when things are being done right (create heroes/sheroes and stories, choose right language)?

- Do our HR systems (hiring, orientation, training, rewards, appraisals, performance management, goal-setting, etc.) support this? If not, what changes must we make?

- How will we reward those who make empowered decisions?

- How will we discourage disempowered behaviors?

As a coach and facilitator, I don't always have all the answers nor am I required to; my clients know their organizations far better than I ever will. These are some of the same questions I have used to get them thinking and really aligning their planning (and eventual execution) around a particular culture component.

2. Availability and Dedication of Resources

According to various research works done over many years, from 44-70 percent of major change initiatives end in failure, often due to poor execution.[172] Did you know that, if people came to work every day and there weren't any new strategies, they would be busy every day, all day? The problem here is one of time and space to focus on the new strategy. People aren't lazy; they are busy! Jim Collins, in his book *Good to Great*

---

[172] (Severini 2013)

Richard Solomon

said, *"the enemy of the great is the good."*[173] If you want a new strategy to get executed, you are going to have to help people make the space and time to do it and stay with it long enough to get the results needed. So how do you keep the 747 in the air and change the engine at the same time?

For the culture change to "stick," enough people need to engage in changed behaviors, see that the organization deems these important, and do them for a sufficiently long enough period of time so that, when there is no prompting or oversight, the actions continue. Just in case you missed it, the sentence above focuses on **behavior**, while our previous definition of culture pointed to norms, beliefs, values, assumptions, legends, and myths. Well, the ultimate evidence of all these is sustained behavior. Let's say it differently: How are we able to know what the values, beliefs, etc., of an organization are? The answer is "based on the behavior of large sections of the organization over the long term.

The Four Disciplines of Execution[174]

I had been a follower of Stephen Covey (deceased 2012) long before his Covey Leadership Center merged with Franklin Quest to become FranklinCovey in 1997. Originally published in 1989, *The 7 Habits of Highly Effective People* has sold over 25 million copies and been translated into 40 languages. In 2004, Dr. Covey followed his mega-successful 7 Habits with *The 8th Habit From Effectiveness to Greatness.*

---

[173] (J. C. Collins 2001)
[174] (McChesney, Covey, and Huling 2016)

Richard Solomon

It must have been around 2008 when I wandered into one of the FranklinCovey retail stores in Washington, D.C., and stumbled onto The 8th Habit, and this was my first encounter with the 4 disciplines of execution. A book by the same name was eventually published in 2012 that fully developed the concepts. I highly recommend you buy a copy and study it like a user manual.

The 4 Disciplines of Execution (called 4DX) is essentially an operating system you can use to achieve your organization's most critical goals (wildly important goals - WIGS). The 4DX is not written as a culture-change nor service-strategy handbook as such. However, in my two decades of experience, it is the best system I have come across for **making space and time**, and creating the focus to execute on the most important **new strategies** that move the organization forward. The disciplines are not intended for the everyday busy work (called the whirlwind). Here is a summary of my understanding of the 4 disciplines of execution and how it can be used to aid with your change efforts. This is just an overview as I cannot do such a work due justice in a few pages.

Discipline 1: Focus on Your Wildly Important Goals (WIGS) [175]

This one has been pretty much covered earlier in this chapter: Narrow your focus and choose one (or two) big goals. In terms of culture change, select one (or two) major culture components — which elements do you believe are most critical to culture change at this time (see culture perspective wheel

---

[175] (McChesney, Covey, and Huling 2016)

Richard Solomon

earlier in this chapter)? Leaders and ambitious types naturally want to go for more wins versus less, but keep in mind that people are already stretched. Based on the law of diminishing returns, you are far more likely to accomplish 1 or 2 goals if you only set and focus on 1 or 2 goals; set 15 goals and you are likely to accomplish zero!

To make it a good goal, you need to ensure that there is a **start line, a finish line, and a deadline.** Without these, all you have is a dream or wish.

Example 1

Let's say you are 25 pounds overweight for your age and height, you might set a goal of: *Lose 10 pounds in the next 30 days or move from 180 pounds to 170 pounds by April 4th 20XX."*

Example 2

Using our earlier example of empowerment, a possible goal could be *"30 percent increase in staff-developed solutions to customer complaints by end of Q2 of 20XX."*

Notice how the goal is stated in measurable terms. There is no way around it; you must have a goal that is measurable, and you know what? Even if you are dealing with behaviors that are more qualitative, most human behaviors can be measured. You may need to get creative to define the behaviors, find a measure, and capture the data, but it is very possible in almost every instance.

Richard Solomon

A client had a challenge: being in the retail optical business, they realized that improved customer engagement in the stores led to increased customer satisfaction and sales volume. The initial challenge was how to measure customer engagement behaviors in the stores. They narrowed it down to speed of greeting; percentage of customers who were greeted, offers of help, and eye contact. Some of these are easier to measure than others, but all can be measured.

Discipline 2: Act on Lead Measures[176]

Typically, when we think of measures, results come to mind; last quarter's performance, the time it took to finish a race, or the number of customers served in an hour. While these are all useful measures, they have one problem in common: They are after-the-fact measurements, and focusing on them won't really improve results. By the time you know what the results are, it's too late; these are what are called lag measures.

Instead, this discipline teaches you to identify and act on the things that have the greatest likelihood of getting you the results you want. Continuing with our examples:

> **Example 1:** *Lose 10 pounds in the next 30 days or move from 180 pounds to 170 pounds by 04th April 20XX."*
>
> **Lead Measures**
> Reduce daily calorie intake by 20 percent.
> Engage in 45 minutes of exercise every other day (4 per week).

---

[176] (McChesney, Covey, and Huling 2016)

Richard Solomon

Example 2: *"30 percent increase in staff-developed solutions to customer complaints by end of Q2 of 20XX."*

Lead Measures

1. All supervisors and managers to ask staff for their ideas about meeting specific customer complaints when they come up (facilitate and coach). – Each manager facilitates a minimum of 10 per week.

2. Supervisors and managers to transfer credibility to staff and express confidence in their ability daily (both to staff and customers).

3. Where errors are made, staff must be coached and trained as needed.

4. Double current decision-making authority levels for all front-liners (e.g. from $50 to $100)

Acting on the lead measures is predictive of the goal outcome or lag measure. If you choose a lead that does not significantly impact the goal, then you need to choose again. Essentially you are making a bet that if you take action on these influenceable factors (the leads), you will get the results you set as your WIG (the lag). [177]

Discipline 3: Create a Compelling Scoreboard[178]

Players play differently when they know the score; if they know they are winning, then they are motivated, exhilarated, and

---

[177] (McChesney, Covey, and Huling 2016)
[178] (McChesney, Covey, and Huling 2016)

Richard Solomon

have a good reason to persist, if they are losing, this is a reason to push harder with the same or changed strategies. The scoreboard is the place you keep track of the lag and lead measures; at any given time, everyone should know exactly where the effort stands. Every department or unit that has a WIG needs a scoreboard.

The best scoreboards are often created by the people who are executing on the actions themselves; they tend to be simple, highly visible to the players, show the current position of the lead and lag measures, and allow people to know at a glance if they are winning or losing.

If the first two disciplines were done right, then it should not be too hard to create a compelling scoreboard. Again from our examples:

Richard Solomon

Infographic 38

Discipline 4: Create a Cadence of Accountability[179]

Accountability is hardly a new concept; business books and circles are filled with references to it. *"People must be held accountable to ensure performance. Who is accountable for these outcomes? Are the accountabilities already in place?"* When you get a new job, one of the earliest discussions is about accountabilities; naturally people do much better when they are held accountable for performance.

As a discipline, this goes beyond good old accountability to creating a "cadence." Cadence comes from the Latin word "cadere" meaning to fall. In English and as it is used here, it has to do with rhythm and timing. Surely you have heard the sound of an old steam engine or locomotive; the timing of the engine can be considered cadence.

Here is how it works:

1. People must make a commitment to doing the most useful 1 – 3 actions based on the lead measures that will impact the scoreboard.

2. A short meeting occurs at least once every week where people report on what they did in the last week to move the scoreboard, and what were the successes and opportunities that still remain.

3. Based on the scoreboard, they decide and commit to what they will do in the coming week (a new commitment).

---

[179] (McChesney, Covey, and Huling 2016)

4. The meetings must happen on a regular interval, which cannot be more than a week.

5. This meeting is only about the wildly important goals (WIGS) versus the normal operational issues.

These meetings can happen more frequently than once per week, but not less; a week is long enough to get some traction on the leads but not so long that people get sucked back into the whirlwind and thus forget the WIGS. Building this cadence takes time and discipline, but once you get it going, it makes a world of difference.

The four disciplines are not difficult, in fact they are simple, which is what makes them so powerful. They are, however, not simplistic. What makes them powerful too is their combination and the magic that happens when they are used consistently. Grab a copy of this book; use the four disciplines (4DX) to move your **signature** service strategy and culture change initiative forward.[180]

Step 8 – Measure, Monitor and Celebrate Early Successes

Just as people need to know the score, they also need to know that they are winning and be rewarded for their efforts. It is crucial to find early wins and celebrate them as soon as possible as this tends to propel people forward and triggers the tendency to persist (motivation). When they see that the desired behaviors are being recognized and celebrated, it creates a new narrative within the

---

[180] (McChesney, Covey, and Huling 2016)

Richard Solomon

organization that we are winning and that going against the (old) status quo is actually welcomed.

Any change effort needs to show early success, remember you are going against the established and reinforced culture that the organization has built up over many years. There need to be as many forces as possible pushing in the opposite direction of the forces that are holding the current culture in place.

A word on monitoring and measurement; what is measured is monitored and what gets monitored gets managed. At the risk of being a bit repetitious: it is critical to have measures for the precious few points of focus so that you can show and know where the effort is heading.[181]

Rewards, Recognition and Reinforcement

A critical component of crafting an organization's culture is ensuring that others see the new behaviors as useful and valuable; it should be clear what we are seeking to create and which behaviors support it. Spend time **catching people doing something right.** Many managers spend a great deal of time and effort looking for and finding "wrong" behaviors; naturally we cannot condone behaviors that work against our vision, but these will need to be coached, trained, and sanctioned (and possibly moved) out. Let's also do some of the opposite; spend time trying to catch people doing something right. Humans work at double the rate to avoid pain versus

---

[181] (Kotter 2012)

gaining pleasure, so make it painful to go in the wrong direction and pleasurable to go in the right.

Painful as used here does not necessarily speak of punishment (at first). Instead, even wrong behaviors should be used as learning opportunities and be coupled with a clear signal that this is not what we want. However we do it, people should not feel scared to think and act, but they should know what the standards of behavior are and what they should avoid.

We should design systems to recognize and reward champions (even small ones) at every level of the organization, and the stories of these sheroes' and heroes' performance should be used to create the folklore which helps build the new culture.

Step 9 - Push on/Don't Let up: The Organization Is Bound to Push Back

The old culture will not go willingly, nor will it roll over and play dead. Remember, people have had years of practice being some other way, so don't for one moment expect that those values, beliefs, and behaviors will just vanish. Instead, you can expect some pushback or resistance at all levels — organizational, team, and individual. Let's look at how this pushback or resistance shows up and some tips on dealing with it.

Individual Level

At the individual level, people have built up habits, and they fear the unknown, are concerned about financial impacts, and general security in changing time.[182] In Chapter 7, I introduced you to the work of neuroscientist Paul D. McLean who indicates that instead of having one brain, humans actually have three. A cross sectional view of the brain shows three distinct structures which are referred to as the lizard brain or the brain stem; the limbic system or emotional brain, and lastly the neocortex (new brain) or analytical brain. [183]

The lizard brain or brain stem is concerned about survival and protection, it reacts in 9/10 of a second and about 95 percent of our decisions are made in this part of our brain. It asks the question, "am I safe?" The emotional brain is the seat of emotions, and governs matters like concern for others, and relationships. It asks the question, "am I loved?" Lastly is the neocortex, the analytical or executive brain, it has a relatively slow reaction time at 1.3 seconds; is responsible for logic, rational thought, and analysis. It asks, "what does this mean?"

When people face changing situations that seem to significantly disturb their status quo, the brain interprets this as a threat; blood flow falls to the neocortex and increases to the emotional and lizard brains. People are thus less rational and analytical and more reactive and emotional. When my way of life is threatened, I will fight back to protect that which is valuable to me.

---

[182] (Kotter 2012)
[183] (MacLean 1990)

Richard Solomon

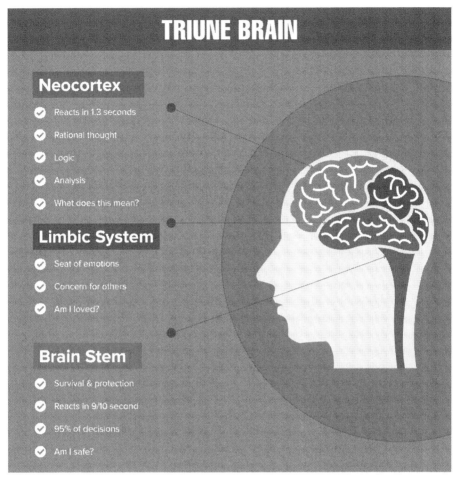

Infographic 39

Here are some strategies to help reduce resistance to change at the individual level:

- Provide both logical and emotional reasons why change is needed, but resist the urge to make logical arguments *only* as many leaders are prone to do.

- Involve and collaborate with others as much as possible – do change *with* people, not *to* them.

Richard Solomon

- Give people time to adjust.

- Provide support and resources, including change-management training.

- Let people talk it out; often resistance ebbs when we have an opportunity to vent because emotions even out. We can then reason things out better.

- Help people see the opportunities in the challenge and what's in it for them; the less they see the change as a threat, the more likely they can think about what's happening and what they can do.

- Will it be easier for people to behave in new ways and harder in old ways? In other words, make sure the organization accommodates the new ways of being.

- Provide knowledge and skill training to increase people's competence and comfort

Group Level

Groups can actually act as barriers to change. Even if an individual wants to change, the group norms may act as a constraint. Remember that people often feel the group forces before those of the organization, and as "herding animals" we generally want to fit in. It is useful to get the whole group involved in the change effort at their level. Another reason for group level resistance is the fear that the group's cohesion or very existence will be threatened. One client I worked with identified **trust** as a crucial cultural element that needed improvement; we facilitated team-building retreats with each team to do the following:

- Identify the trust blockers, some current, some historic.

- Discuss and agree how to overcome them.

- Identify behaviors that were helpful and those that weren't.

- Allay fears that the cohesion and existence of the team will be negatively impacted.

- Identify new norms needed to enhance trust.

- Have initial experience with team trying some of the new actions

- Agree on a plan of action going forward

- Follow-up on the execution of the plan weekly.

Other Group Level Efforts

1. Involve the whole group in developing ideas to support the change.

2. Have them develop their own scoreboard and keep it updated.

3. Encourage key (sometimes unofficial) leaders to be part of the change effort (change army for example).

4. Create healthy intergroup competition if this fits your culture and the change effort (naturally if you are seeking to inject higher levels of collaboration, this may not be a wise idea).

Organizational Level

Inertia is the tendency of a body to remain at rest or continue to move in a straight line. Inertia acts on organizations too, in that the organization *wants* to continue moving along the same path that it has been. This "desire," as it were, is actually built into the systems themselves, as each system and subsystem was created to respond to some stimulus and complete a particular needed task or action for the organization's success.

It is not unusual that a change effort impacts a subsystem but did not fully take into account the larger system; this can create confusion and divided foci. Organizations are different and require different types of adjustment. Here are a few questions I use with some of my own clients:

- Which systems and subsystems support the change we want to create?

- Which systems and subsystems will inhibit the change we want to create?

- What system and subsystem changes must be made?

- Is there alignment among the different systemic changes?

- What messages would help people to embrace and support this change?

- Who should send these messages?

- When and how should these messages be sent?

- Do the systems and subsystems encourage the desired behaviors and discourage the old ways?

- What have we missed?

If your culture is one that generally resists new ideas and holds steady to the status quo, it suggests that it has been designed that way, either intentionally or unintentionally. It also suggests that there are forces that hold this way of being in place. A word of caution: many leaders are accustomed to giving instructions and having them carried out, but culture change is not given to this process. In my experience, leaders give up way too early, either losing the passion for the change or allowing the everyday demands of the organization to take priority. Work for the long term; this is not a sprint.

A **signature** service culture is not an option; it is the absolute best winning strategy an organization can have. Remember that the organization will push back, so don't let up, and overcome the inertia so that the new culture has a chance to take root.

The Secret Sauce

Over the years, I have picked up some tips and tricks that make such a great difference. You already have many of the questions I use with my own clients to help them on their culture-change journeys.

There are two more important elements you should know; these are not steps as such but more frames of reference to ensure that your change efforts are potent. I close this chapter with what could make or break your change effort. Earlier we explored how cultures are formed and how employees learn culture. Let's see how these apply.

Work on the culture (re)formation and culture (re)learning components

As a reminder, here are the culture-formation components we covered previously:

- A clear vision and ideology
- Actions and decisions of founders and other senior leaders
- Selection of staff and training
- Standards

- Rewards and sanctions
- Resource allocation

And the culture-learning components:

- Orientation/socialization of new employees
- Stories
- Heroes and Sheroes
- Rituals and ceremonies
- Material/cultural symbols
- Language and communication
- Managerial decisions

It stands to reason then that if these are how culture is formed and learned, similar attention should be paid to them if you want to change the culture. You should have noticed that all steps and sub-steps in the culture-change process track back to these main components. This is not to say that other steps are not applicable, but I have found it very valuable to work on these through all chosen strategies. You will likely find that most, if not all the strategies you develop will relate or support one of these in some way.

Here are some guidelines based on culture formation and learning:

Formation

- Develop a **clear vision and ideology** of what the new culture or way of being should look like.

- Ensure that the **actions and decisions of founders and other senior leaders** are aligned with the culture you are creating.

Richard Solomon

- **Select new staff** with aligned values and attitudes.

- **Train staff** to manage this and other changes.

- **Train staff** in new skills and knowledge required.

- Set new **standards** for behavior and performance.

- Align **rewards and sanctions** to encourage the behaviors you want and discourage the ones you don't.

- **Allocate resources** for the accomplishment of goals aligned to the culture vision and to show what is truly important.

And the culture learning components:

- **Orient and socialize** new employees in the ways of being, don't leave this to chance.

- Repeatedly **tell stories** about people who are championing the new culture.

- Turn those culture champions into **Heroes and Sheroes** by singing their praises and rewarding them.

- Create **rituals and ceremonies** to show the importance of certain accomplishments and to reinforce them.

- Align **material/cultural symbols** to the kind of culture you are creating.

- **Communicate** using **language** that gives credence to what you want and tells of the new culture. Repeated exposures are needed to make any major change stick, be free to use different or unpopular channels.

- Be sure that **managerial decisions** support the vision, and guard against organizational schizophrenia.

Summary

This entire chapter is a big "what to do section." But for your easy reference, here are the main points again:

1. Have a clear vision of how you want the culture to look.
2. Select, promote and train staff in line with the culture vision.
3. Reward the behaviors you want and sanction those you don't.
4. Ensure that members are deeply socialized in the culture.
5. Teach the new culture
   a. Stories
   b. Heroes and Sheroes
   c. Rituals and ceremonies
   d. Material/cultural symbols
   e. Managerial decisions
6. Identify your own culture change conditions.
7. Use a culture change process.
8. Guard against organizational schizophrenia.
9. Ensure resources are available.
10. Install a new operating system that drives action and holds people accountable.
11. Work *with* resistance
12. Focus on culture (re)formation and (re)learning.

Oh, one last thing for this chapter, I suggest you read it again, there really is a whole lot in here. **Best of luck!** [184]

---

[184] LUCK – Living Under Correct Knowledge

Richard Solomon

Chapter 11

Moving to Action

Alignment – The Hidden Strategy

Organizations are meant to be organized (pun intended); not a disheveled mass of people, processes, and systems working in siloed fashion for some wished-for outcome. Yet, many times I see companies implement strategies in piecemeal fashion, almost hoping that it somehow all fits together. It's like throwing mud against the wall and hoping enough sticks. This can result from several factors:

- A lack of understanding about *how* to lead change or implement new strategies.
- Not thinking it all through.
- Failure to consult the right people.
- A low-collaboration culture that makes it hard for heads to come together.
- Turf protection.
- Hidden agendas and politicking.

I honestly hope you caught it, but just in case you did not, let me make it obvious. Many of the strategies in this book are already being done by your organization in some way. Every organization recruits, has leaders, divides up power, orients, trains, rewards and sanctions behavior, and so on. None of this is new. The hidden or imbedded strategy that we have been covering is actually the alignment (and fine tuning) of all these efforts toward a particular end, in this case, that end is the delivery of **signature** service.

There is a snowballing or cumulative effect that occurs as you begin to repurpose efforts and align them in this way. Even though you may go one or two steps at a time, as you add and align more and more components, you will find that the effort gains momentum at an ever-increasing rate. Staying focused and alignment is key, so do not underestimate or ignore them.

So where to now?

If I were you, at this point I would be asking: "So where exactly do I start?" Quite honestly, I would like to say to you that you should start at step one and then two and on and on. And while you can do this, if yours is like most organizations, the decision may not be so straightforward. Your organization may already have certain pieces firmly in place so there may be little need for working on one component or another.

When writers write and teachers teach, we try to lay out concepts, models, and processes in a step-by-step or linear fashion. While this may work well for some disciplines, when it comes to changing an organization, things don't always work so neatly.

So, what should you do? Which should be your first step? There are some clear guidelines throughout this text; for example, in chapter 4, I said, "leaders go first." In chapter 2, we discussed "making the business case." In chapter 4 we discussed developing a service vision, these are all potent starting points.

Before I get into where you should begin, the infographic below captures all the components of the **signature** service strategy and shows the outcome when each component is missing.

SIGNATURE SERVICE
CULTURE COMPONENTS

Components/Stages								Outcome
Leadership Sponsorship	Service vision	Hire Right	Orientation & Training	Empowerment	Listen to VOC	M3 CX	Craft Culture	Signature Service Culture
	Service vision	Hire Right	Orientation & Training	Empowerment	Listen to VOC	M3 CX	Craft Culture	False Starts
Leadership Sponsorship		Hire Right	Orientation & Training	Empowerment	Listen to VOC	M3 CX	Craft Culture	Misaligned Efforts &Fizzle out
Leadership Sponsorship	Service vision		Orientation & Training	Empowerment	Listen to VOC	M3 CX	Craft Culture	Poor Execution & Performance
Leadership Sponsorship	Service vision	Hire Right		Empowerment	Listen to VOC	M3 CX	Craft Culture	Individual Ideals or Old Culture Prevails
Leadership Sponsorship	Service vision	Hire Right	Orientation & Training		Listen to VOC	M3 CX	Craft Culture	Protectionism (Due to Low Trust) & Bottlenecks
Leadership Sponsorship	Service vision	Hire Right	Orientation & Training	Empowerment		M3 CX	Craft Culture	Lost Bearings & Missed Opportunities
Leadership Sponsorship	Service vision	Hire Right	Orientation & Training	Empowerment	Listen to VOC		Craft Culture	Disjointed Experience Varying Standards of Care
Leadership Sponsorship	Service vision	Hire Right	Orientation & Training	Empowerment	Listen to VOC	M3 CX		Difficult to Create Lasting Change

Infographic 40

Richard Solomon

When Leadership Sponsorship is missing: The effort will not have the authority or resources to succeed. Typically, someone at a lower level sees the need and tries to get the effort moving but won't get very far because they don't have the power or position to sustain the effort; false starts result.

When a Service Vision is missing: Even when people are willing and passionate, they apply their own sense of what should and shouldn't be the focus and priority. Despite how well-intended people are, the lack of an alignment point ends in misaligned efforts and frustrations. Because there is no end-point to shoot for, the effort eventually fizzles out.

When we hire poorly: Much of what goes into **signature** service rests on the attitude and execution of staff and leaders. Hire the wrong people and you are guaranteed failure in terms of execution and performance. Remember how Zappos pays new recruits a bonus of US$2,000 to quit, all in an effort to get the best possible hires?[185] Well Zappos was acquired by Amazon in 2009, and interestingly, Amazon has furthered the approach, taking it beyond new hires to general associates. Called "Pay To Quit," once a year they offer to pay US$2,000 to associates to leave, and the amount goes up annually by US$1,000 with a cap of US$5,000. They want to give employees the opportunity to leave if they (the employees) think they are no longer a good fit. [186]

---

[185] (McFarland 2008)
[186] (White 2014)

Richard Solomon

When orientation and training is lacking: We rely on the goodwill of individuals to work the way they should; instead of being a service machine, individuals' ideas and approaches prevail.

The lack of empowerment: This speaks to low trust, but more than that, it creates severe bottlenecks, as all decisions outside of the policies must be passed up the chain of command for approval. Many more dissatisfied customers leave than necessary.

Failure to listen to the voice of the customer: This results in misguided efforts or lost bearings, as the customer is the only true authority on what the customer wants. Additionally, when we don't listen to the voice of the customer, we are sure to miss opportunities to serve them better with new products and enhanced methods.

When we fail to map, manage, and measure the customer experience: It is likely that the customer will have a disjointed, rather than seamless experience with varying standards of care as they interact with the organization, much of what they experience will be haphazard or hit-and-miss.

Because organizations are systemic, **a lack of focus on culture crafting** can make it extremely hard to create sustainable change, as the system will push back. The trick is to inundate the culture with a multi-pronged, aligned, sustained offensive until it relents and the new way becomes *the way* of being and doing.

All of these are critical, but it is unlikely and actually ill-advised for you to take them all on at the same time. The next section gives some recommendations as to where to begin.

Richard Solomon

Yes, but Where do *I* Start?

The answer to this question depends on where you are now, for very few organizations have the luxury of starting from scratch with a clean slate. If yours is like many of the organizations I have worked with over the years, there are some components included here that you are excellent at and others, not so much.

Essentially, once you have made a business case, you have three options: 1. Go with a classic implementation of one step after the other as I have described throughout this text; 2. Take a piecemeal approach, starting at the weakest point and going from there (based on the **Signature** Culture Perspective Wheel for example); 3. Go with a hybrid of options one and two. I have found the steps below to be most practical and robust in this order:

1. I recommend that you always begin with the elements described in chapter 2 regarding making the business case. This information will come in handy when you need to justify expenditure, get leaders on board, and identify the burning platform.

2. Next, if you know your organization has not even began the service journey in any meaningful way, but it is one given to research and you have the resources, my recommendation is to begin with an assessment of leadership commitment, service vision, empowerment, the voice of the customer and their experience, hiring, orientation, and training. If robust research is not so natural, you can do your own assessment of these factors.

Richard Solomon

3. Are your leaders on board? If you think the answer is yes, how do you know – what is the evidence of their commitment? If the answer is no, then I would suggest you use a business case to help them see what's going on. Then focus on the work in chapter 4 to get them ready to lead and support the effort. If they are already onboard and ready, then you can skip this step.

4. Is the service vision in place? The effort needs a focal point; after leaders being on board and ready, this surely the next port of call.

5. Are you listening to the voice of the customer? Are there systems in place to do this well and regularly? If not, you may want to pay some attention here, as this will guide many of the efforts to follow.

6. From this point on, I suggest you take the culture change route and start with the weakest component (hire right, training and orientation, customer experience, etc.) and go from there.

Keep Improving the Service

Ok, so this book is long enough and longer than I initially intended. If you have made it this far, my sincerest congratulations for staying the course. I am going to keep this short and simple; creating **signature** service is an ongoing job. In fact, the environment is always shifting, and you will find more than enough to keep things interesting. Here are some quick tips for keeping your service on the cutting edge:

Richard Solomon

1. **Listen to your customers**

   Remember, only the customer actually gets to say what is **signature** service – listen to them (and re-read chapter five on the voice of the customer).

2. **Listen to your people**

   Your people interact with customers every day, and they get a firsthand view of what customers want, what they love, and hate. While booking a flight recently, I realized the airline had completely removed the option to select your own seat except until 24 hours before your actual flight!!!! I quickly sent a Facebook message asking why they would take such a retrograde step, and someone responded that I could choose my seats by calling their call center or waiting until 24 hours before my flight!!!!! Had they decided to have open seating, that may have been fine but my brain was asking, "is this 1995?"

   They told me "we would be happy to take your suggestion but for consideration, it must be submitted via a special form" and directed me to an online link to submit it. While I did submit the form (and never received an acknowledgement), I also realized that this company must not take the voice of their front line too seriously. Such a glaring retrograde step should not even require more than the frontline gathering data and passing it to the decision makers.

   Your people should be gathering information based on their interactions with customers and feeding that information into the system so that you can fix problems and grasp opportunities.

3. **Listen to your competition**

   I am sure you are seeing a pattern here; listen, listen, listen! Your competition wants to eat your lunch, so don't ignore them. If they are smaller than you and newer to the market, they may be more nimble and quicker to respond, so pay attention and learn from them. If they are bigger or more entrenched in the industry, they may be more refined and process-driven, so check them out. Don't copy everything, but look for the one nugget among the rocks and sand.

4. **Go Ahead – Refine the Perfection!**

   You may think you have gotten it just right, but you can always refine and improve perfection. Refine the customer experience, take ideas on board, set even higher standards, and go for more. There is always more!

Let's Stay Connected

This book is becoming a movement, be sure to visit our website at *www.thesignatureservicestrategy.com* and sign up to stay up-to-date on all the exciting new things coming out. The inside community is always first to receive new material, trainings, tools, tips, and tricks.

I want to hear from you, go to the website and send me an email. Let me know how your implementation is coming along. I want to celebrate your successes and support you in overcoming the challenges. Send your questions, I will be happy to answer them.

Richard Solomon

Bibliography

A

A. B. C. News. 2015. "Costa Concordia Captain Found Guilty in Fatal Crash." ABC News. February 11, 2015. http://abcnews.go.com/International/costa-concordia-captain-francesco-schettino-found-guilty-fatal/story?id=28894507.

ABC News. 2009. "AOL Buys Time Warner for $162 Billion." ABC News. December 8, 2009. http://abcnews.go.com/Business/Decade/aol-buys-time-warner-162-billion/story?id=9279138.

ABC, News. 2017. "YouTube." https://www.youtube.com/watch?v=pIVrA_SB2pk.

Accenture. 2011. "Accenture 2010 Global Consumer Research Executive Summary." http://www.euroastra.info/files/Accenture_2010_Global_Consumer_Survey_Executive_Summary_v4.pdf.

Airlines, Southwest. 2018. "Purpose, Vision, Values, and Mission." 2018. http://investors.southwest.com/our-company/purpose-vision-values-and-mission.

Allen, James, Frederick Reicheld, Barney Hamilton, and Rob Markey. 2005. "Closing the Delivery Gap." http://www.bain.com/bainweb/pdfs/cms/hotTopics/closingdeliv erygap.pdf.

Amazon. 2018. "Amazon's Global Career Site." Amazon.jobs. 2018. https://www.amazon.jobs/working/working-amazon.

American, Express. 2010. "Global Customer Service Barometer." http://about.americanexpress.com/news/docs/2010x/CSSurvey_ Market_US.pdf.

American, Express. 2012. "2012 Global Customer Service Barometer." http://about.americanexpress.com/news/docs/2012x/axp_2012g csb_us.pdf.

American, Express. 2014. "2014 Global Customer Service Barometer." http://about.americanexpress.com/news/docs/2014x/2014-Global-Customer-Service-Barometer-US.pdf.

Apple Inc. 2017a. "Apple Retail Store - Store List." Apple. 2017. http://www.apple.com/retail/storelist/.

Apple Inc. 2017. "Developer Earnings from the App Store Top $70 Billion." Apple Newsroom. January 6, 2017. https://www.apple.com/newsroom/2017/06/developer-earnings-from-the-app-store-top-70-billion/.

Arthur, Charles. 2012. "RIM 'Could Cut 6,000 Jobs.'" *The Guardian*, May 28, 2012, sec. Technology. http://www.theguardian.com/technology/2012/may/28/rim-to-cut-2000-jobs.

B

Barry, Chris, Rob Markey, Eric Almquist, and Chris Brahm. 2011. "Putting Social Media to Work." September 12, 2011. http://www.bain.com/publications/articles/putting-social-media-to-work.aspx.

BBC, News. 2009. "Singer's Airline Tune Takes off." http://news.bbc.co.uk/2/hi/americas/8164273.stm.

Bell, Chip R., and Ron Zemke. 2013. *Managing Knock Your Socks off Service*. Third Edition. New York: AMACOM - American Management Association.

Bishop, Todd. 2017. "Amazon Soars to More than 341K Employees — Adding More than 110K People in a Single Year." GeekWire. February 2, 2017. https://www.geekwire.com/2017/amazon-soars-340k-employees-adding-110k-people-single-year/.

Bomey, Nathan. 2015. "VW Surpasses Toyota as World's Largest Automaker in First Half of 2015." *USA Today*, July 28, 2015. https://www.usatoday.com/story/money/2015/07/28/volkswagen-surpasses-toyota-worlds-largest-automaker-first-half-2015/30772509/.

Brodkin, Jon. 2012. "No More Cell Phone Minutes? AT&T Expects Data-Only Plans in Two Years." Ars Technica. June 1, 2012. https://arstechnica.com/information-technology/2012/06/no-more-cellphone-minutes-att-expects-data-only-plans-in-two-years/.

Bureau of Transportation Statistics. 2017. "Corrected 2016 Traffic Data for U.S Airlines and Foreign Airlines U.S. Flights | Bureau of Transportation Statistics." March 17, 2017. https://www.rita.dot.gov/bts/press_releases/bts017_17.

Burgess, Matt. 2015. "Internet Growth Is Slowing and Won't Reach 4bn Users until 2020, UN." *Factor* (blog). September 23, 2015. http://factor-tech.com/connected-world/19871-Internet-growth-is-slowing-and-wont-reach-4bn-users-until-2020-un/.

Burke, Collin. 2015. "100 Customer Service Statistics." *InsightSquared* (blog). April 22, 2015. http://www.insightsquared.com/2015/04/100-customer-service-statistics-you-need-to-know/.

Burns, Rebecca. 2012. "New Survey Highlights Importance of Market Research in Building Brand Loyalty." Fourth Source. January 19, 2012. http://www.fourthsource.com/news/new-survey-highlights-importance-of-market-research-in-building-brand-loyalty-5953.

C

Carroll, Dave. 2012. *United Breaks Guitars: The Power of One Voice in the Age of Social Media*. 1st ed. Carlsbad, Calif: Hay House.

Cave, Andrew. 2017. "Culture Eats Strategy For Breakfast. So What's For Lunch?" *Forbes*, November 9, 2017. https://www.forbes.com/sites/andrewcave/2017/11/09/culture-eats-strategy-for-breakfast-so-whats-for-lunch/.

Chan, Calvin. 2016. "Review: 2015 Volkswagen Touareg TDI." 2016. http://www.canadianautoreview.ca/reviews/2015-volkswagen-touareg-tdi.html.

Cisco. 2012. "Cisco's VNI Forecast Projects the Internet Will Be Four Times as Large in Four Years." May 30, 2012. https://newsroom.cisco.com/press-release-content?type=webcontent&articleId=888280.

Richard Solomon

Cisco. 2016. "VNI Complete Forecast Highlights - Global 2020 Forecast Highlights." https://www.cisco.com/c/dam/m/en_us/solutions/service-provider/vni-forecast-highlights/pdf/Global_2020_Forecast_Highlights.pdf.

Cisco. 2017. "Cisco Visual Networking Index: Forecast and Methodology, 2016–2021." Cisco. September 15, 2017. https://www.cisco.com/c/en/us/solutions/collateral/service-provider/visual-networking-index-vni/complete-white-paper-c11-481360.html.

Collins, James C. 2001. *Good to Great: Why Some Companies Make the Leap--and Others Don't.* 1st ed. New York, NY: HarperBusiness.

Collins, Rod. 2015. "Real Business Is About People." *Huffington Post* (blog). November 6, 2015. https://www.huffingtonpost.com/great-work-cultures/real-business-is-about-pe_b_8484486.html.

Colvin, Geoff. 2017. "Lessons From Apple On Making Perfect Products." Fortune. February 17, 2017. http://fortune.com/2017/02/17/3-lessons-from-apple-on-making-perfect-products/.

Corlett, John G., and Carol Pearson. 2003. *Mapping the Organizational Psyche: A Jungian Theory of Organizational Dynamics and Change.* Gainesville, Fla: Center for Applications of Psychological Type.

Richard Solomon

Craggs, Ryan. 2017. "This Airline Gets the Fewest Complaints of Any U.S. Airline." Condé Nast Traveler. April 7, 2017. https://www.cntraveler.com/story/southwest-gets-the-fewest-complaints-of-any-us-airline.

CSM. 2016. "Customer Service Facts." *Customer Service Manager (CSM)*, 2016. https://www.customerservicemanager.com/customer-service-facts/.

D

Deutschendorf, Harvey, and Harvey Deutschendorf. 2015. "Why Emotionally Intelligent People Are More Successful." Fast Company. June 22, 2015. https://www.fastcompany.com/3047455/why-emotionally-intelligent-people-are-more-successful.

Duhigg, Charles, and Keith Bradsher. 2012. "Apple, America and a Squeezed Middle Class." *The New York Times*, January 21, 2012, sec. Business Day. https://www.nytimes.com/2012/01/22/business/apple-america-and-a-squeezed-middle-class.html.

Dumaine, Brian, and Jane Furth. 1993. "TIMES ARE GOOD? CREATE A CRISIS That's What Pepsi-Cola, Ameritech, and Progressive Are Doing to Shake up Their Fat, Happy, and Profitable Organizations before) It's Too Late. Here Are Their Stories. - June 28, 1993." *Fortune Magazine*, June 28, 1993. http://archive.fortune.com/magazines/fortune/fortune_archive/1993/06/28/78005/index.htm.

Richard Solomon

Dunn & Bradstreet, Limited. 2012. "Global Business Failures Report." http://www.dnb.com/content/dam/english/economic-and-industry-insight/global_business_failures_201206.pdf.

E

Econ243. 2017. "Can Apple Continue Its Dominance as a One-Product Company?" Econ243. March 10, 2017. http://econ243.academic.wlu.edu/2017/03/10/can-apple-continue-its-dominance-as-a-one-product-company/.

Egan, Matt. 2015. "HP's Meg Whitman: More Job Cuts Ahead - Jun. 4, 2015." June 4, 2015. http://money.cnn.com/2015/06/04/news/economy/hp-job-cuts-meg-whitman/index.html.

Encyclopedia.com. 2017. "Amazon.com Facts, Information, Pictures | Encyclopedia.com Articles about Amazon.com." 2017. https://www.encyclopedia.com/social-sciences-and-law/economics-business-and-labor/businesses-and-occupations/amazoncom.

energyfacalty.com. 2018. "Primary Energy Consumption." Energyfaculty.com. 2018. https://energyfaculty.com/primary-energy-consumption/.

F

Farrance, Chris. 2002. "EXPERIENCING WORLD CLASS SERVICE EXCELLENCE - US SERVICE EXCELLENCE TOUR NOVEMBER 2001."

Richard Solomon

Fortune. 2017. "The World's Most Admired Companies for 2017." Fortune. 2017. http://fortune.com/worlds-most-admired-companies/.

Freifeld, Lorri. 2016. "Top Spending Trends for Training, 2016-2017." Text. Training Magazine. November 30, 2016. https://trainingmag.com/top-spending-trends-training-2016-2017.

Freire, Axialent. 2007. *Five Archetypes of Culture.* http://ecorner-legacy.stanford.edu/videos/1853/Five-Archetypes-of-Culture.

Fritz, Ben. 2011. "Dish Network Wins Bidding for Assets of Bankrupt Blockbuster." *Los Angles Times*, April 7, 2011. http://articles.latimes.com/2011/apr/07/business/la-fi-ct-dish-blockbuster-20110407.

G

Gallo, Carmine. 2012. "Apple Store's Secret Sauce: 5 Steps of Service [Video]." *Forbes*, May 6, 2012. https://www.forbes.com/sites/carminegallo/2012/05/16/apple-stores-secret-sauce-5-steps-of-service-video/.

Gambrell, Jon. 2012. "Nigeria Fines 4 Mobile Phone Carriers $7.3M." *Associated Press*, May 13, 2012. https://www.yahoo.com/news/nigeria-fines-4-mobile-phone-carriers-7-3m-112624207--finance.html.

Gartner. 2001. "Global Mobile Phone Sales Strong in 2000 but Vendor Challenges Ahead." 2001. https://www.gartner.com/doc/325132/global-mobile-phone-sales-strong.

Gartner. 2012. "Gartner Predicts That Refusing to Communicate by Social Media Will Be as Harmful to Companies as Ignoring Phone Calls or Emails Is Today." August 1, 2012. https://www.gartner.com/newsroom/id/2101515.

Gayomali, Chris. 2011. "Study: 53% of Youngsters Would Choose Technology over Sense of Smell." *Time*, May 27, 2011. http://techland.time.com/2011/05/27/study-53-of-youngsters-would-choose-technology-over-sense-of-smell/.

Genesys. 2009. "The Cost of Poor Customer Service The Economic Impact of the Customer Experience and Engagement in 16 Key Economies." http://www.ancoralearning.com.au/ wp-content/uploads/2014/07/Genesys_Global_Survey09_screen.pdf.

Gesenhues, Amy. 2017. "Report: E-Commerce Accounted for 11.7% of Total Retail Sales in 2016, up 15.6% over 2015." Marketing Land. February 20, 2017. https://marketingland.com/report-e-commerce-accounted-11-7-total-retail-sales-2016-15-6-2015-207088.

Gilligan, Sandra. 2011. "Connecting the Philippines through Mobile Broadband." presented at the Mobile Broadband Regulatory Seminar, The Shangri-La Hotel Makati Philippines, May 10. https://www.gsma.com/spectrum/wp-content/uploads/2012/03/regulatoryseminar.pdf.

Gittell, Jody Hoffer. 2005. *The Southwest Airlines Way: Using the Power of Relationships to Achieve High Performance.* New York: McGraw-Hill.

GSM, Association. 2017. "The Mobile Economy Latin America and the
Caribbean 2017."
https://www.gsmaintelligence.com/research/?file=e14ff2512ee24
4415366a89471bcd3e1&download.

Greelish, David. 2013. "Is There a Walt Disney–Steve Jobs
Connection? | TIME.com." TIME, April 17, 2013.
http://techland.time.com/2013/04/17/is-there-a-walt-
disneysteve-jobs-connection/.

Gulliver. 2015. "Domestic Bliss." *The Economist*, June 24, 2015.
https://www.economist.com/blogs/gulliver/2015/06/worlds-
largest-airlines.

H

Hakimi, Sherry. 2015. "Why Purpose-Driven Companies Are Often
More Successful." July 21, 2015.
https://www.fastcompany.com/3048197/why-purpose-driven-
companies-are-often-more-successful.

Help, Scout. 2017. "These 13 Stories of Remarkable Customer Service
Will Put a Smile on Your Face." Help Scout Blog. 2017.
https://www.helpscout.net/blog/remarkable-customer-service/.

Hesselbein, Frances, and Paul M. Cohen, eds. 1999. *Leader to Leader:
Enduring Insights on Leadership from the Drucker Foundation's
Award-Winning Journal.* San Francisco: Jossey-Bass.

Holson, Laura. 2008. "Sprint Tries to Win Back Disgruntled Phone
Customers." *The New York Times*, July 8, 2008.
http://www.nytimes.com/2008/07/08/business/worldbusiness/
08iht-sprint.1.14323325.html.

Hotten, Russell. 2015. "Volkswagen: The Scandal Explained." *BBC News*, December 10, 2015, sec. Business. http://www.bbc.com/news/business-34324772.

Hughes, Neil. 2015. "Led by Enterprise Sales, Global Tablet Use Predicted to Approach 800M by 2018." AppleInsider. July 13, 2015. //appleinsider.com/articles/15/07/13/led-by-enterprise-sales-global-tablet-use-predicted-to-approach-800m-by-2018.

I

Intelligence, B. I. 2017. "Amazon Accounts for 43% of US Online Retail Sales." Business Insider. February 3, 2017. http://www.businessinsider.com/amazon-accounts-for-43-of-us-online-retail-sales-2017-2.

Isaacson, Walter. 2011. *Steve Jobs*. New York: Simon & Schuster.

J

Jacada. 2008. "Customer Retention Strategies in Action." https://www.jacada.com/images/WhitePapers/pdfs/45.100.0206-Customer-Retention-Strategies.pdf.

K

Kaplan, Marcia. 2017. "Dissecting Amazon's 2016 Financial Performance." *Practical Ecommerce* (blog). February 9, 2017. https://www.practicalecommerce.com/Dissecting-Amazons-2016-Financial-Performance.

Kirkpatrick, James D, and Wendy Kayser Kirkpatrick. 2010. *Training on Trial: How Workplace Learning Must Reinvent Itself to Remain Relevant.* New York: AMACOM. http://www.books24x7.com/marc.asp?bookid=32487.

Kotter, John P. 2012. "Accelerate!" *Harvard Business Review,* November 1, 2012. https://hbr.org/2012/11/accelerate.

L

Lampton, Ph. D, Bill. 2003. "'My Pleasure' - The Ritz-Carlton Hotel Part II." *Expert Magazine,* December 1, 2003. http://www.expertmagazine.com/artman/publish/printer_391.shtml.

LeBoeuf, Michael. 2000. *How to Win Customers and Keep Them for Life: Revised and Updated for the Digital Age.* Berkley rev. trade pbk. ed. New York: Berkley Books.

Limited, Massy Motors Automotive. 2018. "Massy Motors - About." 2018. http://massymotors.com/motors/pages/about.aspx.

Lloyd, Matt. 2016. "Customers Will Love You For This." MOBE - My Own Business Education. February 29, 2016. https://mobe.com/customers-will-love-you-for-this/.

M

MacGillavry, Kim, and Pa Sinyan. 2016. "Focusing on the Critical Link Between Employee Engagement and Customer Centricity at DHL Freight." *Global Business and Organizational Excellence* 35 (4): 6–16. https://doi.org/10.1002/joe.21680.

MacLean, Paul D. 1990. *The Triune Brain in Evolution: Role in Paleocerebral Functions.* New York: Plenum Press.

Richard Solomon

Malik, Om. 2011. "Internet of Things Will Have 24 Billion Devices by 2020." October 13, 2011. https://gigaom.com/2011/10/13/Internet-of-things-will-have-24-billion-devices-by-2020/.

Marriott, J. Willard. 1997. *The Spirit to Serve: Marriott's Way*. New York: HarperCollins.

Martins, Flavio. 2015. "Demystifying Ritz-Carlton Legendary Customer Service." *Win the Customer!* (blog). January 29, 2015. http://winthecustomer.com/demystifying-ritz-carlton-secret-legendary-customer-service/.

Maxwell, John C. 2007. *The 21 Irrefutable Laws of Leadership: Follow Them and People Will Follow You*. Rev. and updated 10th anniversary ed. Nashville, Tenn: Thomas Nelson.

McChesney, Chris, Sean Covey, and Jim Huling. 2016. *The 4 Disciplines of Execution: Achieving Your Wildly Important Goals*.

McFarland, Keith. 2008. "Why Zappos Offers New Hires $2,000 to Quit." *Business Week*, September 17, 2008. http://hrpeople.monster.com/news/articles/1251-why-zappos-offers-new-hires-2000-to-quit?print=true.

Merced, Michael de la. 2010. "Blockbuster Files for Chapter 11 Bankruptcy." *The New York Times*, September 23, 2010. http://www.nytimes.com/2010/09/24/business/24blockbuster.html.

Merced, Michael de la. 2015. "Pfizer and Allergan Reach $150 Billion Merger Deal - *The New York Times*." The New York Times, November 22, 2015. https://www.nytimes.com/2015/11/23/business/dealbook/pfizer-and-allergan-reach-150-billion-merger-deal.html.

Michaels, Dave. 2010. "White House Seeks Customer Service Advice from Southwest Airlines' Gary Kelly." *The Dallas Morning News*, January 15, 2010. https://www.southwestaircommunity.com/t5/Southwest-Stories/White-House-seeks-customer-service-advice-from-Southwest/ba-p/1808.

Michelli, Joseph A. 2008. *The New Gold Standard: 5 Leadership Principles for Creating a Legendary Customer Experience Courtesy of the Ritz-Carlton Hotel Company.* New York: McGraw-Hill.

Michelli, Joseph A. 2012. The Zappos Experience: 5 Principles to Inspire, Engage, and Wow. New York: McGraw-Hill.

Mickiewicz, Mark. 2011. "Why Customer Service Is The New Marketing." *Forbes*, December 28, 2011. https://www.forbes.com/sites/theyec/2011/12/28/why-customer-service-is-the-new-marketing/#4d308b8f5fb1.

Mickiewicz, Matt. 2009. "How Zappos Does Customer Service and Company Culture." *Sitepoint.* https://www.sitepoint.com/how-zappos-does-customer-service-and-company-culture/.

Mindock, Clark. 2017. "United Airlines Reaches Settlement with David Dao after Doctor Was Violently Dragged off Flight | The Independent." *Independent*, April 27, 2017. http://www.independent.co.uk/news/business/news/united-airlines-settlement-david-dao-passenger-dragged-off-flight-video-a7706591.html.

Richard Solomon

Molla, Rani. 2017. "Amazon Could Be Responsible for Nearly Half of U.S. E-Commerce Sales in 2017." Recode. October 24, 2017. https://www.recode.net/2017/10/24/16534100/amazon-market-share-ebay-walmart-apple-ecommerce-sales-2017.

Moore, Michael. 2017. "BlackBerry Phones Are in REAL Trouble, and This Is Why." *Express.co.uk*, April 4, 2017. https://www.express.co.uk/pictures/pics/9934/new-blackberry-mercury-android-smartphone-ces-2017.

Murphy Jr., Bill. 2015. "20 Great Quotes About Finding Happiness (Richard Branson Edition)," October 8, 2015. https://www.inc.com/bill-murphy-jr/20-great-quotes-about-finding-happiness-richard-branson-edition.html.

Murphy, Julia, and Max Roser. 2018. "Internet." https://ourworldindata.org/Internet.

N

Nasdaq. 2018. "NASDAQ's Homepage for Retail Investors." NASDAQ.com. 2018. http://www.nasdaq.com/.

Nasir, Süphan. 2015. *Customer Relationship Management Strategies in the Digital Era.* A Volume in the Advances in Marketing, Customer Relationship Management, and E-Services (AMCRMES) Book Series. Hershey: Business Science Reference, An Imprint of IGI Global.

O

Ostrow, Adam. 2011. "Netflix Cuts Customer Forecast By 1 Million as Price Hike Takes Effect." Mashable. September 15, 2011. http://mashable.com/2011/09/15/netflix-customers/.

P

Parature, Inc. 2010. "Lessons in Loyalty: How Southwest Airlines Does It – An Insider's Point of View." http://www.lessonsinloyalty.com/ParatureWhitePage.pdf.

Picchi, Aimee. 2017. "United Ranks as America's Bottom-Rated Legacy Airline." April 25, 2017. https://www.cbsnews.com/news/united-ranks-as-americas-bottom-rated-legacy-airline/.

Pilzer, Paul Zane. 1990. *Unlimited Wealth: The Theory and Practice of Economic Alchemy*. 1st ed. New York: Crown Publishers.

Pinsker, Joe. 2014. "The Psychology Behind Costco's Free Samples." *The Atlantic*, October 1, 2014. https://www.theatlantic.com/business/archive/2014/10/the-psychology-behind-costcos-free-samples/380969/.

Point, Topic. 2014. "Point Topic - Global Fixed Broadband Subscriber Forecasts to Dec 2020." Point Topic. 2014. http://point-topic.com/free-analysis/global-fixed-broadband-subscriber-forecasts-to-dec-2020/.

Poushter, Jacob. 2016. "Smartphone Ownership and Internet Usage Continues to Climb in Emerging Economies." *Pew Research Center's Global Attitudes Project* (blog). February 22, 2016. http://www.pewglobal.org/2016/02/22/smartphone-ownership-and-Internet-usage-continues-to-climb-in-emerging-economies/.

Richard Solomon

Q

Qualman, Erik. 2013. Socialnomics: *How Social Media Transforms the Way We Live and Do Business*. Second edition. Hoboken, New Jersey: John Wiley & Sons, Inc.

R

Rasmus, Daniel W. 2012. *"Defining Your Company's Vision."* Fast Company. February 28, 2012. https://www.fastcompany.com/1821021/defining-your-companys-vision.

Reichheld, Frederick. 2000. "The Economics of E-Loyalty." *HBS Working Knowledge*, July 12, 2000. http://hbswk.hbs.edu/archive/1590.htmlthe-economics-of-e-loyalty.

Reichheld, Frederick F., and Jr W. Earl Sasser. 1990. "Zero Defections: Quality Comes to Services." *Harvard Business Review*, September 1, 1990. https://hbr.org/1990/09/zero-defections-quality-comes-to-services.

Ritz-Carlton, The. 2017. "Luxury Hotels & Resorts." The Ritz-Carlton. 2017. http://www.ritzcarlton.com/en/about/gold-standards.

Robbins, Stephen P. 2001. *Organizational Behavior*. 9th ed. Upper Saddle River, N.J: Prentice Hall.

Robbins, Stephen P., and Tim Judge. 2013. *Organizational Behavior*. 15th ed. Boston: Pearson.

Rodriguez, Donna, Rita Patel, Andrea Bright, Donna Gregory, and Marilyn K. Gowing. 2002. "Developing Competency Models to Promote Integrated Human Resource Practices." *Human*

Resource Management 41 (3): 309–24.
https://doi.org/10.1002/hrm.10043.

Rose, Kevin. 2015. "'Netflix and Chill': the Complete History of a Viral Sex Catchphrase." 2015. https://splinternews.com/netflix-and-chill-the-complete-history-of-a-viral-sex-1793850444.

S

Schein, Edgar. 1992. *Organizational Culture & Leadership.* Jossey-Bass.

Severini, Gail. 2013. "Time to Kill the Phantom 70% Failure Rate Quoted on Transformational Strategy?" *Change Whisperer - Gail Severini, Symphini Change Management Inc.* (blog). November 16, 2013. https://gailseverini.com/2013/11/16/time-to-kill-the-phantom-70-failure-rate-quoted-on-transformational-strategy/.

Shepardson, David, and Alana Wise. 2017. "U.S. Lawmakers Grill Airline Executives after Customer Disasters." *Reuters*, May 3, 2017. https://www.reuters.com/article/us-ual-passenger-ceo/united-ceo-takes-responsibility-for-passenger-incident-idUSKBN17Y1J8.

Sons of Maxwell. 2009. *YouTube.* https://www.youtube.com/watch?v=5YGc4zOqozo.

Southwest Airlines. 2017a. "Awards." Southwest Airlines Newsroom. 2017. https://www.swamedia.com//pages/awards.

Southwest Airlines. 2017. "Southwest Airlines Reports Fourth Quarter And Record Annual Profit; 44th Consecutive Year Of Profitability." 2017. http://www.southwestairlinesinvestorrelations.com/news-and-events/news-releases/2017/01-26-2017-111504198.

Richard Solomon

Southwest Airlines. 2018. "Labor Contracts." Southwest Airlines Newsroom. 2018. https://www.swamedia.com//pages/contracts.

Statista. 2017a. "Global E-Commerce Share of Retail Sales 2021 | Statistic." Statista. 2017. https://www.statista.com/statistics/534123/e-commerce-share-of-retail-sales-worldwide/.

Statista. 2017. "Global Retail E-Commerce Market Size 2014-2021." Statista. 2017. https://www.statista.com/statistics/379046/worldwide-retail-e-commerce-sales/.

Statista. 2018. "Car Production: Number of Cars Produced Worldwide 2016." Statista. 2018. https://www.statista.com/statistics/262747/worldwide-automobile-production-since-2000/. https://www.statista.com/statistics/262747/worldwide-automobile-production-since-2000/.

Statistic, Brain. 2017. "Computer Sales Statistics – Statistic Brain." 2017. https://www.statisticbrain.com/computer-sales-statistics/.

Sullenberger, Chesley, and Jeffrey Zaslow. 2009. *Highest Duty: My Search for What Really Matters*. 1st ed. New York: William Morrow.

T

The Gleaner, Company. 2016. "Liberty Global Completes Acquisition of Cable and Wireless Plc." *The Gleaner*, May 16, 2016. http://jamaica-gleaner.com/article/lead-stories/20160516/liberty-global-completes-acquisition-cable-and-wireless-plc.

Richard Solomon

Think, Customer. 2008. "Survey: Customer Churn Rate Rises by 15 Percent | CustomerThink." February 4, 2008. http://customerthink.com/hike_customer_churn_rate_15/.

Thomas, Lauren. 2017. "This Chart Shows How Quickly Amazon Is 'Eating the Retail World.'" July 7, 2017. https://www.cnbc.com/2017/07/07/amazon-is-eating-the-retail-world.html.

Thompson, Arthur A., and Arthur A. Thompson, eds. 2012. *Crafting and Executing Strategy: The Quest for Competitive Advantage: Concepts and Cases.* 18th ed. New York: McGraw-Hill/Irwin.

Tillman, Karen. 2013. "How Many Internet Connections Are in the World? Right. Now." blogs@Cisco - Cisco Blogs. July 29, 2013. https://blogs.cisco.com/news/cisco-connections-counter.

Trevail, Charles. 2016. "It's Time to Rethink the Chief Customer Officer Role | Guest Columnists - AdAge." 2016. http://adage.com/article/digitalnext/rethinking-chief-customer-officer/303146/.

Tschohl, John. 2011. *Achieving Excellence through Customer Service.* Minneapolis, Minn.: Best Sellers Pub.

U

Udland, Myles. 2017. "United Airlines Loses $950 Million in Market Value as Shares Tumble." April 11, 2017. https://finance.yahoo.com/news/united-airlines-shares-tumbling-140648573.html.

Richard Solomon

V

Vanian, Jonathan. 2017. "HPE CEO Meg Whitman Explains Why She's Stepping Down | Fortune." *Fortune*, November 22, 2017. http://fortune.com/2017/11/21/meg-whitman-hewlett-packard-enterprise-ceo/.

W

White, Martha. 2014. "Amazon Will Pay You $5,000 to Quit Your Job." *Time*, April 11, 2014. http://time.com/58305/amazon-will-pay-you-5000-to-quit-your-job/.

Whittaker, Zack, and Roger Cheng. 2012. "HP Plans to Cut 27,000 Jobs, Plow Savings into R&D - CNET." May 23, 2012. https://www.cnet.com/news/hp-plans-to-cut-27000-jobs-plow-savings-into-r-d/.

Wolfe, Chaundera. 2012. "RightNow’s Annual Research Shows 86 Percent of U.S. Adults Will Pay More For A Better Customer Experience." January 11, 2012. http://www.businesswire.com/news/home/20120111005284/en/RightNow%E2%80%99s-Annual-Research-Shows-86-Percent-U.S.

World Economic, Forum. 2017. "Global Risks of Highest Concern for Doing Business 2017." *Global Risks Report 2017* (blog). 2017. http://wef.ch/2izYjIJ.

wwwMOXNEWScom. 2017. *CEO Of United Airlines GRILLED On Their Treatment Of Passengers By Members Of Congress!* https://www.youtube.com/watch?v=5IZ4y3DyDuA.

Z

Zappos.com. 2017. "About Zappos." 2017.
    https://www.zappos.com/about/home.

Zappos.com. 2018. "About Zappos Culture | Zappos.com." 2018.
    https://www.zappos.com/core-values.

Zemke, Ron, and Chip R. Bell. 2000. *Knock Your Socks off Service Recovery*. New York: AMACOM.

About the Author

Richard Dick Solomon is the Principal Consultant and Managing Director of **Development Consulting Center Limited.**

He holds post-graduate degrees in Organization Transformation and Strategic Human Resource Management and has over 25 years experience in Organization Development. As a change architect and strategist, he specializes in **Signature** Service, leadership development and change.

As a global speaker, coach, trainer and consultant, Richard supports the development of individuals and organizations in over 36 countries. His client list includes Fortune 500 (global) companies like 3M, Nestle, General Electric, IBM, PepsiCo, Coca-Cola, BP, Vodafone, Unilever, AIG, GlaxoSmithKline, Royal Bank of Canada, and Fujitsu.

He holds memberships at the NTL Institute of Applied Human Behavior, the Association of Training and Development and The Human Resource Management Association of Trinidad and Tobago. Richard sits on several boards and management committees including the Trinidad and Tobago Scout Association, the PRVM Performing Arts Academy and the Programme for Development and Training at the Commonwealth Telecommunications Organization in the United Kingdom.

Richard is listed in the **"Who's Who in Trinidad and Tobago Business"** and has lectured Management and Human Resource Management.

11663567R00177

Made in the USA
Lexington, KY
13 October 2018